Workshop on Applications of Tree Automata in Natural Language Processing 2010

(ATANLP 2010)

Held at ACL 2010

Uppsala, Sweden
16 July 2010

ISBN: 978-1-61738-809-5

Printed from e-media with permission by:

Curran Associates, Inc.
57 Morehouse Lane
Red Hook, NY 12571

CURRAN ASSOCIATES INC. proceedings.com

Some format issues inherent in the e-media version may also appear in this print version.

Printed by Curran Associates, Inc. (2010)

Association for Computational Linguistics
209 N. Eighth Street
Stroudsburg, Pennsylvania 18360

Phone: 1-570-476-8006
Fax: 1-570-476-0860

acl@aclweb.org

Additional copies of this publication are available from:

Curran Associates, Inc.
57 Morehouse Lane
Red Hook, NY 12571 USA
Phone: 845-758-0400
Fax: 845-758-2634
Email: curran@proceedings.com
Web: www.proceedings.com

Preface

We are pleased to present the proceedings of the ACL 2010 Workshop on Applications of Tree Automata in Natural Language Processing, which will be held on July 16 in Uppsala, Sweden, following the 48th Annual Meeting of the Association for Computational Linguistics (ACL).

The theory of tree automata has always had a close connection with natural language processing. In the 1960s, computational linguistics was the major driving force for the development of a theory of tree automata. However, the number of successful applications of this theory to natural language processing remained small during the 20th century. This situation has now changed. Applications of tree automata in natural language processing can be found in work on topics as diverse as grammar formalisms, computational semantics, language generation, and machine translation. Researchers in natural language processing have recognized the usefulness of tree automata theory for solving the problems they are interested in, and theorists are inspired by the resulting theoretical questions.

The goals of this workshop are to provide a dedicated venue for the presentation of work that relates the theory of tree automata to natural language processing, and to create a forum where researchers from the two areas can meet and exchange ideas. Specifically, the workshop aims at raising the awareness for theoretical results useful for applications in natural language processing, and at identifying open theoretical problems raised by such applications.

We are very happy that Kevin Knight (ISI/University of Southern California, USA), certainly the most recognized ambassador for tree automata techniques in machine translation, agreed to give one of his stimulating invited lectures.

For the workshop, authors were invited to submit full papers and proposals for quickfire presentations, the latter being a means for triggering discussions and an exchange of ideas. After a thorough reviewing process with three reviews per full paper, six full papers and four quickfire presentations were accepted for the workshop. The quality and diversity of the papers accepted ensures an interesting and inspiring workshop that we look forward to.

We thank the members of the program committee for their support, and in particular for being careful reviewers of the papers submitted. Furthermore, we would like to thank the program chairs, Sandra Carberry and Stephen Clark, as well as the workshop chairs, Pushpak Bhattacharyia and David Weir, for their friendly and professional assistance.

We hope that all participants of the workshop will experience an inspiring event characterized by curiosity and an open-minded atmosphere, and that all readers of these proceedings will gain new insights that make a difference.

Frank Drewes
Marco Kuhlmann

May 2010

Organizers:

Frank Drewes, Umeå University, Sweden
Marco Kuhlmann, Uppsala University, Sweden

Program Committee:

Parosh Aziz Abdulla, Uppsala University, Sweden
Leonor Becerra-Bonache, Yale University, USA
Chris Callison-Burch, Johns Hopkins University, USA
David Chiang, ISI/University of Southern California, USA
Loek Cleophas, University of Pretoria, South Africa, and Eindhoven University of Technology, the Netherlands
Trevor Cohn, University of Sheffield, UK
François Denis, Université de Provence, France
Johanna Högberg, Umeå University, Sweden
Liang Huang, ISI/University of Southern California, USA
Stephan Kepser, codecentric AG, Germany
Alexander Koller, Saarland University, Germany
Andreas Maletti, Universitat Rovira i Virgili, Spain
Sebastian Maneth, NICTA and University of New South Wales, Australia
Jonathan May, ISI/University of Southern California, USA
Brink van der Merwe, University of Stellenbosch, South Africa
Mark-Jan Nederhof, University of St Andrews, UK
Joachim Niehren, INRIA, France
Kai Salomaa, Queen's University, Canada
Anoop Sarkar, Simon Fraser University, Canada
Giorgio Satta, University of Padua, Italy
Stuart Shieber, Harvard University, USA
Magnus Steinby, University of Turku, Finland
Marc Tommasi, INRIA, France
Heiko Vogler, Technische Universität Dresden, Germany

Invited Speaker:

Kevin Knight, ISI/University of Southern California, USA

Table of Contents

Workshop Program

Friday, July 16, 2010

09:00–09:15 Opening Remarks

09:15–10:30 Invited Talk by Kevin Knight

10:30–11:00 Coffee Break

Full Paper Session 1

11:00–11:30 *Preservation of Recognizability for Synchronous Tree Substitution Grammars*
Zoltán Fülöp, Andreas Maletti and Heiko Vogler

11:30–12:00 *A Decoder for Probabilistic Synchronous Tree Insertion Grammars*
Steve DeNeefe, Kevin Knight and Heiko Vogler

12:00–12:30 *Parsing and Translation Algorithms Based on Weighted Extended Tree Transducers*
Andreas Maletti and Giorgio Satta

12:30–14:00 Lunch Break

Full Paper Session 2

14:00–14:30 *Millstream Systems – a Formal Model for Linking Language Modules by Interfaces*
Suna Bensch and Frank Drewes

14:30–15:00 *Transforming Lexica as Trees*
Mark-Jan Nederhof

15:00–15:30 *n-Best Parsing Revisited*
Matthias Büchse, Daniel Geisler, Torsten Stüber and Heiko Vogler

15:30–16:00 Coffee Break

Friday, July 16, 2010 (continued)

Quickfire Presentations

16:00–16:15 *Tree Automata Techniques and the Learning of Semantic Grammars*
Michael Minock

16:15–16:30 *Do We Really Want a Single Tree to Cover the Whole Sentence?*
Aravind Joshi

16:30–16:45 *The Tree Automata Workbench 'Marbles'*
Frank Drewes

16:45–17:00 *Requirements on a Tree Transformation Model for Machine Translation*
Andreas Maletti

17:00–17:30 Discussion

Preservation of Recognizability for Synchronous Tree Substitution Grammars

Zoltán Fülöp
Department of Computer Science
University of Szeged
Szeged, Hungary

Andreas Maletti
Departament de Filologies Romàniques
Universitat Rovira i Virgili
Tarragona, Spain

Heiko Vogler
Faculty of Computer Science
Technische Universität Dresden
Dresden, Germany

Abstract

We consider synchronous tree substitution grammars (STSG). With the help of a characterization of the expressive power of STSG in terms of weighted tree bimorphisms, we show that both the forward and the backward application of an STSG preserve recognizability of weighted tree languages in all reasonable cases. As a consequence, both the domain and the range of an STSG without chain rules are recognizable weighted tree languages.

1 Introduction

The syntax-based approach to statistical machine translation (Yamada and Knight, 2001) becomes more and more competitive in machine translation, which is a subfield of natural language processing (NLP). In this approach the full parse trees of the involved sentences are available to the translation model, which can base its decisions on this rich structure. In the competing phrase-based approach (Koehn et al., 2003) the translation model only has access to the linear sentence structure.

There are two major classes of syntax-based translation models: *tree transducers* and *synchronous grammars*. Examples in the former class are the top-down tree transducer (Rounds, 1970; Thatcher, 1970), the extended top-down tree transducer (Arnold and Dauchet, 1982; Galley et al., 2004; Knight and Graehl, 2005; Graehl et al., 2008; Maletti et al., 2009), and the extended multi bottom-up tree transducer (Lilin, 1981; Engelfriet et al., 2009; Maletti, 2010). The latter class contains the syntax-directed transductions of Lewis II and Stearns (1968), the generalized syntax-directed transductions (Aho and Ullman, 1969), the synchronous tree substitution grammar (STSG) by Schabes (1990) and the synchronous tree adjoining grammar (STAG) by Abeillé et al. (1990) and Shieber and Schabes (1990). The first bridge between those two classes were established in (Martin and Vere, 1970). Further comparisons can be found in (Shieber, 2004) for STSG and in (Shieber, 2006) for STAG.

One of the main challenges in NLP is the ambiguity that is inherent in natural languages. For instance, the sentence *"I saw the man with the telescope"* has several different meanings. Some of them can be distinguished by the parse tree, so that probabilistic parsers (Nederhof and Satta, 2006) for natural languages can (partially) achieve the disambiguation. Such a parser returns a set of parse trees for each input sentence, and in addition, each returned parse tree is assigned a likelihood. Thus, the result can be seen as a mapping from parse trees to probabilities where the impossible parses are assigned the probability 0. Such mappings are called weighted tree languages, of which some can be finitely represented by weighted regular tree grammars (Alexandrakis and Bozapalidis, 1987). Those weighted tree languages are *recognizable* and there exist algorithms (Huang and Chiang, 2005) that efficiently extract the k-best parse trees (i.e., those with the highest probability) for further processing.

In this paper we consider synchronized tree substitution grammars (STSG). To overcome a technical difficulty we add (grammar) nonterminals to them. Since an STSG often uses the nonterminals of a context-free grammar as terminal symbols (i.e., its derived trees contain both terminal and nonterminal symbols of the context-free grammar), we call the newly added (grammar) nonterminals of the STSG *states*. Substitution does no longer take place at synchronized nonterminals (of the context-free grammar) but at synchronized states (one for the input and one for the output side). The states themselves will not appear in the final derived trees, which yields that it is sufficient to assume that only identical states are synchro-

Proceedings of the 2010 Workshop on Applications of Tree Automata in Natural Language Processing, ACL 2010, pages 1–9,
Uppsala, Sweden, 16 July 2010. ©2010 Association for Computational Linguistics

nized. Under those conventions a rule of an STSG has the form $q \to (s, t, V, a)$ where q is a state, $a \in \mathbb{R}_{\geq 0}$ is the rule weight, s is an input tree that can contain states at the leaves, and t is an output tree that can also contain states. Finally, the synchronization is defined by V, which is a bijection between the state-labeled leaves of s and t. We require that V only relates identical states.

The rules of an STSG are applied in a step-wise manner. Here we use a derivation relation to define the semantics of an STSG. It can be understood as the synchronization of the derivation relations of two regular tree grammars (Gécseg and Steinby, 1984; Gécseg and Steinby, 1997) where the synchronization is done on nonterminals (or states) in the spirit of syntax-directed transductions (Lewis II and Stearns, 1968). Thus each sentential form is a pair of (nonterminal-) connected trees.

An STSG $\mathcal{G}$ computes a mapping $\tau_{\mathcal{G}}$, called its weighted tree transformation, that assigns a weight to each pair of input and output trees, where both the input and output tree may not contain any state. This transformation is obtained as follows: We start with two copies of the initial state that are synchronized. Given a connected tree pair (ξ, ζ), we can apply the rule $q \to (s, t, V, a)$ to each pair of synchronized states q. Such an application replaces the selected state q in ξ by s and the corresponding state q in ζ by t. All the remaining synchronized states and the synchronized states of V remain synchronized. The result is a new connected tree pair. This step charges the weight a. The weights of successive applications (or steps) are multiplied to obtain the weight of the derivation. The weighted tree transformation $\tau_{\mathcal{G}}$ assigns to each pair of trees the sum of all weights of derivations that derive that pair.

Shieber (2004) showed that for every classical unweighted STSG there exists an equivalent bimorphism (Arnold and Dauchet, 1982). The converse result only holds up to deterministic relabelings (Gécseg and Steinby, 1984; Gécseg and Steinby, 1997), which remove the state information from the input and output tree. It is this difference that motivates us to add states to STSG. We generalize the result of Shieber (2004) and prove that every weighted tree transformation that is computable by an STSG can also be computed by a weighted bimorphism and vice versa.

Given an STSG and a recognizable weighted tree language φ of input trees, we investigate under which conditions the weighted tree language obtained by applying $\mathcal{G}$ to φ is again recognizable. In other words, we investigate under which conditions the forward application of $\mathcal{G}$ preserves recognizability. The same question is investigated for backward application, which is the corresponding operation given a recognizable weighted tree language of output trees. Since STSG are symmetric (i.e., input and output can be exchanged), the results for backward application can be obtained easily from the results for forward application.

Our main result is that forward application preserves recognizability if the STSG $\mathcal{G}$ is output-productive, which means that each rule of $\mathcal{G}$ contains at least one output symbol that is not a state. Dually, backward application preserves recognizability if $\mathcal{G}$ is input-productive, which is the analogous property for the input side. In fact, those results hold for weights taken from an arbitrary commutative semiring (Hebisch and Weinert, 1998; Golan, 1999), but we present the results only for probabilities.

2 Preliminary definitions

In this contribution we will work with *ranked trees*. Each symbol that occurs in such a tree has a fixed rank that determines the number of children of nodes with this label. Formally, let Σ be a *ranked alphabet*, which is a finite set Σ together with a mapping $\mathrm{rk}_\Sigma \colon \Sigma \to \mathbb{N}$ that associates a rank $\mathrm{rk}_\Sigma(\sigma)$ with every $\sigma \in \Sigma$. We let $\Sigma_k = \{\sigma \in \Sigma \mid \mathrm{rk}_\Sigma(\sigma) = k\}$ be the set containing all symbols in Σ that have rank k. A Σ-*tree* indexed by a set Q is a tree with nodes labeled by elements of $\Sigma \cup Q$, where the nodes labeled by some $\sigma \in \Sigma$ have exactly $\mathrm{rk}_\Sigma(\sigma)$ children and the nodes with labels of Q have no children. Formally, the set $T_\Sigma(Q)$ of (term representations of) Σ-trees indexed by a set Q is the smallest set T such that

- $Q \subseteq T$ and
- $\sigma(t_1, \dots, t_k) \in T$ for every $\sigma \in \Sigma_k$ and $t_1, \dots, t_k \in T$.

We generally write α instead of $\alpha()$ for all $\alpha \in \Sigma_0$.

We frequently work with the set $\mathrm{pos}(t)$ of *positions* of a Σ-tree t, which is defined as follows. If $t \in Q$, then $\mathrm{pos}(t) = \{\varepsilon\}$, and if $t = \sigma(t_1, \dots, t_k)$, then

$$\mathrm{pos}(t) = \{\varepsilon\} \cup \{iw \mid 1 \leq i \leq k, w \in \mathrm{pos}(t_i)\} \ .$$

Thus, each position is a finite (possibly empty) sequence of natural numbers. Clearly, each position designates a node of the tree, and vice versa. Thus we identify nodes with positions. As usual, a *leaf* is a node that has no children. The set of all leaves of t is denoted by $\mathrm{lv}(t)$. Clearly, $\mathrm{lv}(t) \subseteq \mathrm{pos}(t)$.

The label of a position $w \in \mathrm{pos}(t)$ is denoted by $t(w)$. Moreover, for every $A \subseteq \Sigma \cup Q$, let $\mathrm{pos}_A(t) = \{w \in \mathrm{pos}(t) \mid t(w) \in A\}$ and $\mathrm{lv}_A(t) = \mathrm{pos}_A(t) \cap \mathrm{lv}(t)$ be the sets of positions and leaves that are labeled with an element of A, respectively. Let $t \in T_\Sigma(Q)$ and $w_1, \dots, w_k \in \mathrm{lv}_Q(t)$ be k (pairwise) different leaves. We write $t[w_1 \leftarrow t_1, \dots, w_k \leftarrow t_k]$ or just $t[w_i \leftarrow t_i \mid 1 \leq i \leq k]$ with $t_1, \dots, t_k \in T_\Sigma(Q)$ for the tree obtained from t by replacing, for every $1 \leq i \leq k$, the leaf w_i with the tree t_i.

For the rest of this paper, let Σ and Δ be two arbitrary ranked alphabets. To avoid consistency issues, we assume that a symbol σ that occurs in both Σ and Δ has the same rank in Σ and Δ; i.e., $\mathrm{rk}_\Sigma(\sigma) = \mathrm{rk}_\Delta(\sigma)$. A *deterministic relabeling* is a mapping $r \colon \Sigma \to \Delta$ such that $r(\sigma) \in \Delta_k$ for every $\sigma \in \Sigma_k$. For a tree $s \in T_\Sigma$, the relabeled tree $r(s) \in T_\Delta$ is such that $\mathrm{pos}(r(s)) = \mathrm{pos}(s)$ and $\big(r(s)\big)(w) = r(s(w))$ for every $w \in \mathrm{pos}(s)$. The class of tree transformations computed by deterministic relabelings is denoted by dREL.

A tree language (over Σ) is a subset of T_Σ. Correspondingly, a *weighted tree language* (over Σ) is a mapping $\varphi \colon T_\Sigma \to \mathbb{R}_{\geq 0}$. A *weighted tree transformation* (over Σ and Δ) is a mapping $\tau \colon T_\Sigma \times T_\Delta \to \mathbb{R}_{\geq 0}$. Its *inverse* is the weighted tree transformation $\tau^{-1} \colon T_\Delta \times T_\Sigma \to \mathbb{R}_{\geq 0}$, which is defined by $\tau^{-1}(t, s) = \tau(s, t)$ for every $t \in T_\Delta$ and $s \in T_\Sigma$.

3 Synchronous tree substitution grammars with states

Let Q be a finite set of *states* with a distinguished *initial state* $q_S \in Q$. A *connected tree pair* is a tuple (s, t, V, a) where $s \in T_\Sigma(Q)$, $t \in T_\Delta(Q)$, and $a \in \mathbb{R}_{\geq 0}$. Moreover, $V \colon \mathrm{lv}_Q(s) \to \mathrm{lv}_Q(t)$ is a bijective mapping such that $s(u) = t(v)$ for every $(u, v) \in V$. We will often identify V with its graph. Intuitively, a connected tree pair (s, t, V, a) is a pair of trees (s, t) with a weight a such that each node labeled by a state in s has a corresponding node in t, and vice versa. Such a connected tree pair (s, t, V, a) is *input-productive* and *output-productive* if $s \notin Q$ and $t \notin Q$, respectively. Let Conn denote the set of all connected tree pairs that use the index set Q. Moreover, let $\mathrm{Conn}_\mathrm{p} \subseteq \mathrm{Conn}$ contain all connected tree pairs that are input- or output-productive.

A *synchronous tree substitution grammar $\mathcal{G}$ (with states) over Σ, Δ, and Q* (for short: STSG), is a finite set of *rules* of the form $q \to (s, t, V, a)$ where $q \in Q$ and $(s, t, V, a) \in \mathrm{Conn}_\mathrm{p}$. We call a rule $q \to (s, t, V, a)$ a *q-rule*, of which q and (s, t, V, a) are the *left-hand* and *right-hand side*, respectively, and a is its *weight*. The STSG $\mathcal{G}$ is *input-productive* (respectively, *output-productive*) if each of its rules is so. To simplify the following development, we assume (without loss of generality) that two different q-rules differ on more than just their weight.[1]

To make sure that we do not account essentially the same derivation twice, we have to use a deterministic derivation mode. Since the choice is immaterial, we use the leftmost derivation mode for the output component t of a connected tree pair (s, t, V, a). For every $(s, t, V, a) \in \mathrm{Conn}$ such that $V \neq \emptyset$, the *leftmost output position* is the pair $(w, w') \in V$, where w' is the leftmost (i.e., the lexicographically smallest) position of $\mathrm{lv}_Q(t)$.

Next we define derivations. The *derivation relation induced by $\mathcal{G}$* is the binary relation $\Rightarrow_\mathcal{G}$ over Conn such that

$$\xi = (s_1, t_1, V_1, a_1) \Rightarrow_\mathcal{G} (s_2, t_2, V_2, a_2) = \zeta$$

if and only if the leftmost output position of ξ is $(w, w') \in V_1$ and there exists a rule

$$s_1(w) \to (s, t, V, a) \in \mathcal{G}$$

such that

- $s_2 = s_1[w \leftarrow s]$ and $t_2 = t_1[w' \leftarrow t]$,
- $V_2 = (V_1 \setminus \{(w, w')\}) \cup V'$ where $V' = \{(ww_1, w'w_2) \mid (w_1, w_2) \in V\}$, and
- $a_2 = a_1 \cdot a$.

A sequence $D = (\xi_1, \dots, \xi_n) \in \mathrm{Conn}^n$ is a *derivation* of $(s, t, V, a) \in \mathrm{Conn}$ from $q \in Q$ if

- $\xi_1 = (q, q, \{(\varepsilon, \varepsilon)\}, 1)$,
- $\xi_n = (s, t, V, a)$, and
- $\xi_i \Rightarrow_\mathcal{G} \xi_{i+1}$ for every $1 \leq i \leq n - 1$.

The set of all such derivations is denoted by $D^q_\mathcal{G}(s, t, V, a)$.

For every $q \in Q$, $s \in T_\Sigma(Q)$, $t \in T_\Delta(Q)$, and bijection $V \colon \mathrm{lv}_Q(s) \to \mathrm{lv}_Q(t)$, let

$$\tau^q_\mathcal{G}(s, t, V) = \sum_{a \in \mathbb{R}_{\geq 0}, D \in D^q_\mathcal{G}(s,t,V,a)} a \enspace .$$

[1]Formally, $q \to (s, t, V, a) \in G$ and $q \to (s, t, V, b) \in G$ implies $a = b$.

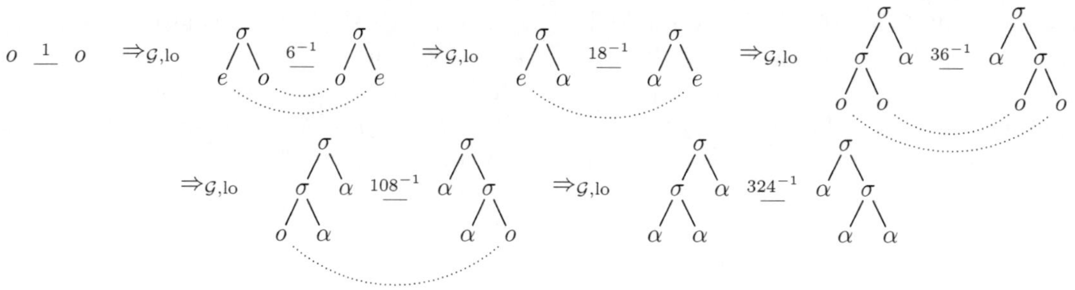

Figure 1: Example derivation with the STSG $\mathcal{G}$ of Example 1.

Finally, the *weighted tree transformation computed by* $\mathcal{G}$ is the weighted tree transformation $\tau_{\mathcal{G}} : T_\Sigma \times T_\Delta \to \mathbb{R}_{\geq 0}$ with $\tau_{\mathcal{G}}(s,t) = \tau_{\mathcal{G}}^{q_S}(s,t,\emptyset)$ for every $s \in T_\Sigma$ and $t \in T_\Delta$. As usual, we call two STSG equivalent if they compute the same weighted tree transformation. We observe that every STSG is essentially a linear, nondeleting weighted extended top-down (or bottom-up) tree transducer (Arnold and Dauchet, 1982; Graehl et al., 2008; Engelfriet et al., 2009) without (both-sided) epsilon rules, and vice versa.

Example 1. *Let us consider the* STSG $\mathcal{G}$ *over* $\Sigma = \Delta = \{\sigma, \alpha\}$ *and* $Q = \{e, o\}$ *where* $q_S = o$, $\mathrm{rk}(\sigma) = 2$, *and* $\mathrm{rk}(\alpha) = 0$. *The* STSG $\mathcal{G}$ *consists of the following rules where* $V = \{(1,2),(2,1)\}$ *and* $\mathrm{id} = \{(1,1),(2,2)\}$*:*

$$o \to (\sigma(o,e), \sigma(e,o), V, 1/3) \qquad (\rho_1)$$
$$o \to (\sigma(e,o), \sigma(o,e), V, 1/6) \qquad (\rho_2)$$
$$o \to (\sigma(e,o), \sigma(e,o), \mathrm{id}, 1/6) \qquad (\rho_3)$$
$$o \to (\alpha, \alpha, \emptyset, 1/3) \qquad (\rho_4)$$
$$e \to (\sigma(e,e), \sigma(e,e), V, 1/2) \qquad (\rho_5)$$
$$e \to (\sigma(o,o), \sigma(o,o), V, 1/2) \qquad (\rho_6)$$

Figure 1 shows a derivation induced by $\mathcal{G}$. *It can easily be checked that* $\tau_{\mathcal{G}}(s,t) = \frac{1}{6 \cdot 3 \cdot 2 \cdot 3 \cdot 3}$ *where* $s = \sigma(\sigma(\alpha,\alpha),\alpha)$ *and* $t = \sigma(\alpha, \sigma(\alpha,\alpha))$. *Moreover,* $\tau_{\mathcal{G}}(s,s) = \tau_{\mathcal{G}}(s,t)$. *If* $\tau_{\mathcal{G}}^q(s,t,\emptyset) \neq 0$ *with* $q \in \{e,o\}$, *then* s *and* t *have the same number of* α*-labeled leaves. This number is odd if* $q = o$, *otherwise it is even. Moreover, at every position* $w \in \mathrm{pos}(s)$, *the left and right subtrees* s_1 *and* s_2 *are interchanged in* s *and* t *(due to* V *in the rules* $\rho_1, \rho_2, \rho_5, \rho_6$*) except if* s_1 *and* s_2 *contain an even and odd number, respectively, of* α*-labeled leaves. In the latter case, the subtrees can be interchanged or left unchanged (both with probability* $1/6$*).*

4 Recognizable weighted tree languages

Next, we recall weighted regular tree grammars (Alexandrakis and Bozapalidis, 1987). To keep the presentation simple, we identify WRTG with particular STSG, in which the input and the output components are identical. More precisely, a *weighted regular tree grammar over* Σ *and* Q (for short: WRTG) is an STSG $\mathcal{G}$ over Σ, Σ, and Q where each rule has the form $q \to (s, s, \mathrm{id}, a)$ where id is the suitable (partial) identity mapping. It follows that $s \notin Q$, which yields that we do not have chain rules. In the rest of this paper, we will specify a rule $q \to (s,s,\mathrm{id},a)$ of a WRTG simply by $q \xrightarrow{a} s$. For every $q \in Q$, we define the weighted tree language $\varphi_{\mathcal{G}}^q : T_\Sigma(Q) \to \mathbb{R}_{\geq 0}$ *generated by* $\mathcal{G}$ *from* q by $\varphi_{\mathcal{G}}^q(s) = \tau_{\mathcal{G}}^q(s, s, \mathrm{id}_{\mathrm{lv}_Q(s)})$ for every $s \in T_\Sigma(Q)$, where $\mathrm{id}_{\mathrm{lv}_Q(s)}$ is the identity on $\mathrm{lv}_Q(s)$. Moreover, the weighted tree language $\varphi_{\mathcal{G}} : T_\Sigma \to \mathbb{R}_{\geq 0}$ *generated by* $\mathcal{G}$ is defined by $\varphi_{\mathcal{G}}(s) = \varphi_{\mathcal{G}}^{q_S}(s)$ for every $s \in T_\Sigma$.

A weighted tree language $\varphi : T_\Sigma \to \mathbb{R}_{\geq 0}$ is *recognizable* if there exists a WRTG $\mathcal{G}$ such that $\varphi = \varphi_{\mathcal{G}}$. We note that our notion of recognizability coincides with the classical one (Alexandrakis and Bozapalidis, 1987; Fülöp and Vogler, 2009).

Example 2. *We consider the* WRTG $\mathcal{K}$ *over the input alphabet* $\Sigma = \{\sigma, \alpha\}$ *and* $P = \{p, q\}$ *with* $q_S = q$, $\mathrm{rk}(\sigma) = 2$, *and* $\mathrm{rk}(\alpha) = 0$. *The* WRTG $\mathcal{K}$ *contains the following rules:*

$$q \xrightarrow{0.4} \sigma(p, \alpha) \quad q \xrightarrow{0.6} \alpha \quad p \xrightarrow{1} \sigma(\alpha, q) \quad (\nu_1\text{–}\nu_3)$$

Let $s \in T_\Sigma$ *be such that* $\varphi_{\mathcal{K}}(s) \neq 0$. *Then* s *is a thin tree with zig-zag shape; i.e., there exists* $n \geq 1$ *such that* $\mathrm{pos}(s)$ *contains exactly the positions:*

- $(12)^i$ *for every* $0 \leq i \leq \lfloor \frac{n-1}{2} \rfloor$, *and*
- $(12)^i 1$, $(12)^i 2$, *and* $(12)^i 11$ *for every integer* $0 \leq i \leq \lfloor \frac{n-3}{2} \rfloor$.

The integer n *can be understood as the length of a derivation that derives* s *from* q. *Some example*

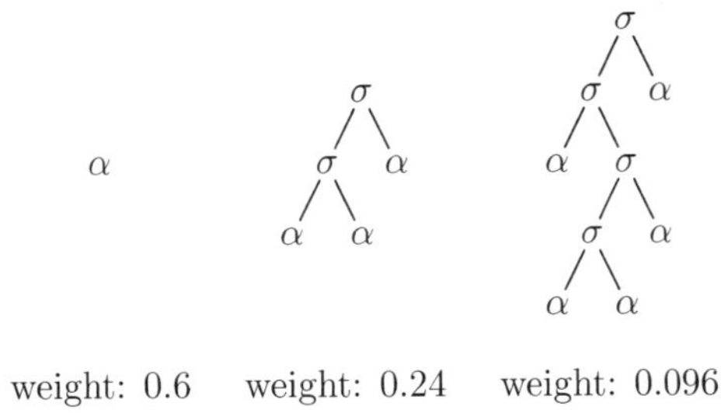

Figure 2: Example trees and their weight in $\varphi_\mathcal{G}$ where $\mathcal{G}$ is the WRTG of Example 2.

trees with their weights are displayed in Figure 2.

Proposition 3. *For every* WRTG $\mathcal{G}$ *there is an equivalent* WRTG $\mathcal{G}'$ *in* normal form, *in which the right-hand side of every rule contains exactly one symbol of* Σ.

Proof. We can obtain the statement by a trivial extension to the weighted case of the approach used in Lemma II.3.4 of (Gécseg and Steinby, 1984) and Section 6 of (Gécseg and Steinby, 1997). □

5 STSG and weighted bimorphisms

In this section, we characterize the expressive power of STSG in terms of weighted bimorphisms. This will provide a conceptually clear pattern for the construction in our main result (see Theorem 6) concerning the closure of recognizable weighted tree languages under forward and backward application. For this we first recall tree homomorphisms. Let Γ and Σ be two ranked alphabets. Moreover, let $h\colon \Gamma \to T_\Sigma \times (\mathbb{N}^*)^*$ be a mapping such that $h(\gamma) = (s, u_1, \ldots, u_k)$ for every $\gamma \in \Gamma_k$ where $s \in T_\Sigma$ and all leaves $u_1, \ldots, u_k \in \mathrm{lv}(s)$ are pairwise different. The mapping h induces the (linear and complete) *tree homomorphism* $\widetilde{h}\colon T_\Gamma \to T_\Sigma$, which is defined by $\widetilde{h}(\gamma(d_1, \ldots, d_k)) = s[u_1 \leftarrow \widetilde{d_1}, \ldots, u_k \leftarrow \widetilde{d_k}]$ for every $\gamma \in \Gamma_k$ and $d_1, \ldots, d_k \in T_\Gamma$ with $h(\gamma) = (s, u_1, \ldots, u_k)$ and $\widetilde{d_i} = \widetilde{h}(d_i)$ for every $1 \le i \le k$. Moreover, every (linear and complete) tree homomorphism is induced in this way. In the rest of this paper we will not distinguish between h and $\widetilde{h}$ and simply write h instead of $\widetilde{h}$. The homomorphism h is *order-preserving* if $u_1 < \cdots < u_k$ for every $\gamma \in \Gamma_k$ where $h(\gamma) = (s, u_1, \ldots, u_k)$. Finally, we note that every $\tau \in \mathrm{dREL}$ can be computed by a order-preserving tree homomorphism.

A *weighted bimorphism* $\mathcal{B}$ *over* Σ *and* Δ consists of a WRTG $\mathcal{K}$ over Γ and P and two tree homomorphisms

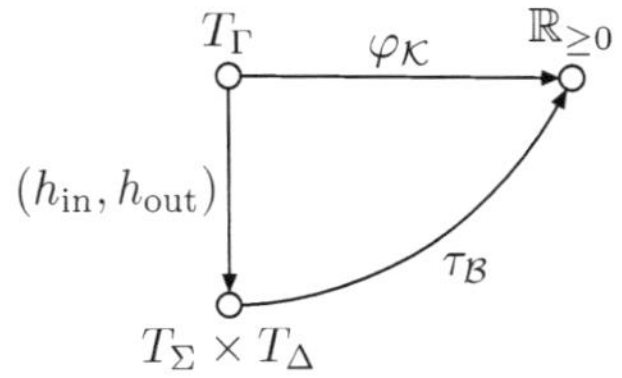

Figure 3: Illustration of the semantics of the bimorphism $\mathcal{B}$.

$$h_{\mathrm{in}}\colon T_\Gamma \to T_\Sigma \quad \text{and} \quad h_{\mathrm{out}}\colon T_\Gamma \to T_\Delta \ .$$

The bimorphism $\mathcal{B}$ *computes* the weighted tree transformation $\tau_\mathcal{B}\colon T_\Sigma \times T_\Delta \to \mathbb{R}_{\ge 0}$ with

$$\tau_\mathcal{B}(s, t) = \sum_{d \in h_{\mathrm{in}}^{-1}(s) \cap h_{\mathrm{out}}^{-1}(t)} \varphi_\mathcal{K}(d)$$

for every $s \in T_\Sigma$ and $t \in T_\Delta$.

Without loss of generality, we assume that every bimorphism $\mathcal{B}$ is presented by an WRTG $\mathcal{K}$ in normal form and an order-preserving output homomorphism h_{out}. Next, we prepare the relation between STSG and weighted bimorphisms. Let $\mathcal{G}$ be an STSG over Σ, Δ, and Q. Moreover, let $\mathcal{B}$ be a weighted bimorphism over Σ and Δ consisting of (i) $\mathcal{K}$ over Γ and P in normal form, (ii) h_{in}, and (iii) order-preserving h_{out}. We say that $\mathcal{G}$ and $\mathcal{B}$ are *related* if $Q = P$ and there is a bijection $\theta\colon \mathcal{G} \to \mathcal{K}$ such that, for every rule $\rho \in \mathcal{G}$ with $\rho = (q \to (s, t, V, a))$ and $\theta(\rho) = (p \xrightarrow{a} \gamma(p_1, \ldots, p_k))$ we have

- $p = q$,
- $h_{\mathrm{in}}(\gamma) = (s, u_1, \ldots, u_k)$,
- $h_{\mathrm{out}}(\gamma) = (t, v_1, \ldots, v_k)$,
- $V = \{(u_1, v_1), \ldots, (u_k, v_k)\}$, and
- $s(u_i) = p_i = t(v_i)$ for every $1 \le i \le k$.

Let $\mathcal{G}$ and $\mathcal{B}$ be related. The following three easy statements can be used to prove that $\mathcal{G}$ and $\mathcal{B}$ are equivalent:

1. For every derivation $D \in D^q_\mathcal{G}(s, t, \emptyset, a)$ with $q \in Q, s \in T_\Sigma, t \in T_\Delta, a \in \mathbb{R}_{\ge 0}$, there exists $d \in T_\Gamma$ and a derivation $D' \in D^q_\mathcal{K}(d, d, \emptyset, a)$ such that $h_{\mathrm{in}}(d) = s$ and $h_{\mathrm{out}}(d) = t$.
2. For every $d \in T_\Gamma$ and $D' \in D^q_\mathcal{K}(d, d, \emptyset, a)$ with $q \in Q$ and $a \in \mathbb{R}_{\ge 0}$, there exists a derivation $D \in D^q_\mathcal{G}(h_{\mathrm{in}}(d), h_{\mathrm{out}}(d), \emptyset, a)$.
3. The mentioned correspondence on derivations is a bijection.

Given an STSG $\mathcal{G}$, we can easily construct a weighted bimorphism $\mathcal{B}$ such that $\mathcal{G}$ and $\mathcal{B}$ are related, and vice versa. Hence, STSG and weighted bimorphisms are equally expressive, which generalizes the corresponding characterization result in the unweighted case by Shieber (2004), which we will state after the introduction of STSG$\downarrow$.

Classical synchronous tree substitution grammars (STSG$\downarrow$) do not have states. An STSG$\downarrow$ can be seen as an STSG by considering every substitution site (i.e., each pair of synchronised nonterminals) as a state.[2] We illustrate this by means of an example here. Let us consider the STSG$\downarrow$ $\mathcal{G}$ with the following rules:

- $(S(\alpha, B\downarrow), S(D\downarrow, \beta))$ with weight 0.2
- $(B(\gamma, B\downarrow), D(\delta, D\downarrow))$ with weight 0.3
- $(B(\alpha), D(\beta))$ with weight 0.4.

The substitution sites are marked with $\downarrow$. Any rule with root A can be applied to a substitution site $A\downarrow$. An equivalent STSG $\mathcal{G}'$ has the rules:

$$\begin{aligned}&\langle S, S\rangle \to (S(\alpha, \langle B, D\rangle), S(\langle B, D\rangle, \beta), V, 0.2)\\&\langle B, D\rangle \to (B(\gamma, \langle B, D\rangle), D(\delta, \langle B, D\rangle), V', 0.3)\\&\langle B, D\rangle \to (B(\alpha), D(\beta), \emptyset, 0.4)\ ,\end{aligned}$$

where $V = \{(2, 1)\}$ and $V' = \{(2, 2)\}$. It is easy to see that $\mathcal{G}$ and $\mathcal{G}'$ are equivalent.

Let $\Sigma = \{\gamma, \gamma', \gamma'', \alpha, \beta\}$ where $\gamma, \gamma', \gamma'' \in \Sigma_1$ and $\alpha, \beta \in \Sigma_0$ (and $\gamma' \neq \gamma''$ and $\alpha \neq \beta$). We write $\gamma^m(t)$ with $t \in T_\Sigma$ for the tree $\gamma(\cdots\gamma(t)\cdots)$ containing m occurrences of γ above t. STSG$\downarrow$ have a certain locality property, which yields that STSG$\downarrow$ cannot compute transformations like

$$\tau(s, t) = \begin{cases}1 & \text{if } s = \gamma'(\gamma^m(\alpha)) = t\\ & \text{or } s = \gamma''(\gamma^m(\beta)) = t\\ 0 & \text{otherwise}\end{cases}$$

for every $s, t \in T_\Sigma$. The non-local feature is the correspondence between the symbols γ' and α (in the first alternative) and the symbols γ'' and β (in the second alternative). An STSG that computes τ is presented in Figure 4.

Theorem 4. *Let τ be a weighted tree transformation. Then the following are equivalent.*

1. *τ is computable by an* STSG.
2. *τ is computable by a weighted bimorphism.*
3. *There exists a* STSG$\downarrow$ *$\mathcal{G}$ and deterministic relabelings r_1 and r_2 such that*

$$\tau(s, t) = \sum_{s' \in r_1^{-1}(s), t' \in r_2^{-1}(t)} \tau_{\mathcal{G}}(s', t')\ .$$

[2] To avoid a severe expressivity restriction, several initial states are allowed for an STSG$\downarrow$.

The inverse of an STSG computable weighted tree transformation can be computed by an STSG. Formally, the *inverse* of the STSG $\mathcal{G}$ is the STSG

$$\mathcal{G}^{-1} = \{(t, s, V^{-1}, a) \mid (s, t, V, a) \in \mathcal{G}\}$$

where V^{-1} is the inverse of V. Then $\tau_{\mathcal{G}^{-1}} = \tau_{\mathcal{G}}^{-1}$.

6 Forward and backward application

Let us start this section with the definition of the concepts of forward and backward application of a weighted tree transformation $\tau \colon T_\Sigma \times T_\Delta \to \mathbb{R}_{\geq 0}$ to weighted tree languages $\varphi \colon T_\Sigma \to \mathbb{R}_{\geq 0}$ and $\psi \colon T_\Delta \to \mathbb{R}_{\geq 0}$. We will give general definitions first and deal with the potentially infinite sums later. The *forward application* of τ to φ is the weighted tree language $\tau(\varphi) \colon T_\Delta \to \mathbb{R}_{\geq 0}$, which is defined for every $t \in T_\Delta$ by

$$\big(\tau(\varphi)\big)(t) = \sum_{s \in T_\Sigma} \varphi(s) \cdot \tau(s, t)\ . \qquad (1)$$

Dually, the *backward application* of τ to ψ is the weighted tree language $\tau^{-1}(\psi) \colon T_\Sigma \to \mathbb{R}_{\geq 0}$, which is defined for every $s \in T_\Sigma$ by

$$\big(\tau^{-1}(\psi)\big)(s) = \sum_{t \in T_\Delta} \tau(s, t) \cdot \psi(t)\ . \qquad (2)$$

In general, the sums in Equations (1) and (2) can be infinite. Let us recall the important property that makes them finite in our theorems.

Proposition 5. *For every input-productive (resp., output-productive)* STSG *$\mathcal{G}$ and every tree $s \in T_\Sigma$ (resp., $t \in T_\Delta$), there exist only finitely many trees $t \in T_\Delta$ (respectively, $s \in T_\Sigma$) such that $\tau_{\mathcal{G}}(s, t) \neq 0$.*

Proof sketch. If $\mathcal{G}$ is input-productive, then each derivation step creates at least one input symbol. Consequently, any derivation for the input tree s can contain at most as many steps as there are nodes (or positions) in s. Clearly, there are only finitely many such derivations, which proves the statement. Dually, we can obtain the statement for output-productive STSG. □

In the following, we will consider forward applications $\tau_{\mathcal{G}}(\varphi)$ where $\mathcal{G}$ is an output-productive STSG and φ is recognizable, which yields that (1) is well-defined by Proposition 5. Similarly, we consider backward applications $\tau_{\mathcal{G}}^{-1}(\psi)$ where $\mathcal{G}$ is input-productive and ψ is recognizable, which again yields that (2) is well-defined by Proposition 5. The question is whether $\tau_{\mathcal{G}}(\varphi)$ and $\tau_{\mathcal{G}}^{-1}(\psi)$

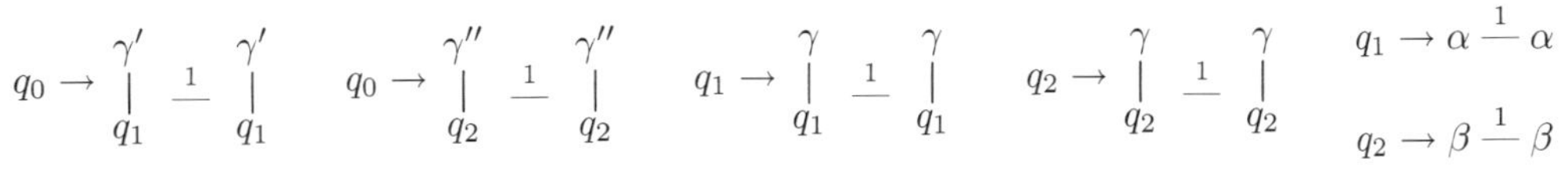

Figure 4: STSG computing the weighted tree transformation τ with initial state q_0.

are again recognizable. To avoid confusion, we occasionally use angled parentheses as in $\langle p, q \rangle$ instead of standard parentheses as in (p, q). Moreover, for ease of presentation, we identify the initial state q_S with $\langle q_S, q_S \rangle$.

Theorem 6. *Let $\mathcal{G}$ be an* STSG *over Σ, Δ, and Q. Moreover, let $\varphi \colon T_\Sigma \to \mathbb{R}_{\geq 0}$ and $\psi \colon T_\Delta \to \mathbb{R}_{\geq 0}$ be recognizable weighted tree languages.*

1. *If $\mathcal{G}$ is output-productive, then $\tau_\mathcal{G}(\varphi)$ is recognizable.*
2. *If $\mathcal{G}$ is input-productive, then $\tau_\mathcal{G}^{-1}(\psi)$ is recognizable.*

Proof. For the first item, let $\mathcal{K}$ be a WRTG over Σ and P such that $\varphi = \varphi_\mathcal{K}$. Without loss of generality, we suppose that $\mathcal{K}$ is in normal form.

Intuitively, we take each rule $q \to (s, t, V, a)$ of $\mathcal{G}$ and run the WRTG $\mathcal{K}$ with every start state p on the input side s of the rule. In this way, we obtain a weight b. The WRTG will reach the state leaves of s in certain states, which we then transfer to the linked states in t to obtain t'. Finally, we remove the input side and obtain a rule $\langle p, q \rangle \stackrel{ab}{\to} t'$ for the WRTG $\mathcal{L}$ that represents the forward application. We note that the same rule of $\mathcal{L}$ might be constructed several times. If this happens, then we replace the several copies by one rule whose weight is the sum of the weights of all copies. As already mentioned the initial state is $\langle q_S, q_S \rangle$. Clearly, this approach is inspired (and made reasonable) by the bimorphism characterization. We can take the HADAMARD product of the WRTG of the bimorphism with the inverse image of $\varphi_\mathcal{K}$ under its input homomorphism. Then we can simply project to the output side. Our construction performs those three steps at once. The whole process is illustrated in Figure 5.

Formally, we construct the WRTG $\mathcal{L}$ over Δ and $P \times Q$ with the following rules. Let $p \in P$, $q \in Q$, and $t' \in T_\Delta(P \times Q)$. Then $\langle p, q \rangle \stackrel{c}{\to} t'$ is a rule in $\mathcal{L}'$, where

$$c = \sum_{\substack{(q \to (s,t,V,a)) \in \mathcal{G} \\ V = \{(u_1,v_1),\dots,(u_k,v_k)\} \\ p_1,\dots,p_k \in P \\ t' = t[v_i \leftarrow \langle p_i, t(v_i)\rangle \mid 1 \leq i \leq k] \\ b = \varphi_\mathcal{K}^p(s[u_i \leftarrow p_i \mid 1 \leq i \leq k])}} ab \enspace .$$

This might create infinitely many rules in $\mathcal{L}'$, but clearly only finitely many will have a weight different from 0. Thus, we can obtain the finite rule set $\mathcal{L}$ by removing all rules with weight 0.

The main statement to prove is the following: for every $t \in T_\Delta(Q)$ with $\mathrm{lv}_Q(t) = \{v_1, \dots, v_k\}$, $p, p_1, \dots, p_k \in P$, and $q \in Q$

$$\sum_{\substack{s \in T_\Sigma(Q) \\ u_1,\dots,u_k \in \mathrm{lv}_Q(s)}} \varphi_\mathcal{K}^p(s') \cdot \tau_\mathcal{G}^q(s, t, V) = \varphi_\mathcal{L}^{\langle p,q \rangle}(t') \enspace ,$$

where

- $V = \{(u_1, v_1), \dots, (u_k, v_k)\}$,
- $s' = s[u_i \leftarrow p_i \mid 1 \leq i \leq k]$, and
- $t' = t[v_i \leftarrow \langle p_i, t(v_i) \rangle \mid 1 \leq i \leq k]$.

In particular, for $t \in T_\Delta$ we obtain

$$\sum_{s \in T_\Sigma} \varphi_\mathcal{K}^p(s) \cdot \tau_\mathcal{G}^q(s, t, \emptyset) = \varphi_\mathcal{L}^{\langle p,q \rangle}(t) \enspace ,$$

which yields

$$\begin{aligned} \big(\tau_\mathcal{G}(\varphi_\mathcal{K})\big)(t) &= \sum_{s \in T_\Sigma} \varphi_\mathcal{K}(s) \cdot \tau_\mathcal{G}(s, t) \\ &= \sum_{s \in T_\Sigma} \varphi_\mathcal{K}^{q_S}(s) \cdot \tau_\mathcal{G}^{q_S}(s, t, \emptyset) \\ &= \varphi_\mathcal{L}^{\langle q_S, q_S \rangle}(t) = \varphi_\mathcal{L}(t) \enspace . \end{aligned}$$

In the second item $\mathcal{G}$ is input-productive. Then $\mathcal{G}^{-1}$ is output-productive and $\tau_\mathcal{G}^{-1}(\psi) = \tau_{\mathcal{G}^{-1}}(\psi)$. Hence the first statement proves that $\tau_\mathcal{G}^{-1}(\psi)$ is recognizable. □

Example 7. *As an illustration of the construction in Theorem 6, let us apply the* STSG *$\mathcal{G}$ of Example 1 to the* WRTG *$\mathcal{K}$ over Σ and $P = \{p, q_S, q_\alpha\}$ and the following rules:*

$$q_S \stackrel{\frac{2}{5}}{\to} \sigma(p, q_\alpha) \qquad q_S \stackrel{\frac{3}{5}}{\to} \alpha$$
$$p \stackrel{1}{\to} \sigma(q_\alpha, q_S) \qquad q_\alpha \stackrel{1}{\to} \alpha \enspace .$$

In fact, $\mathcal{K}$ is in normal form and is equivalent to the WRTG *of Example 2. Using the construction in the proof of Theorem 6 we obtain the* WRTG *$\mathcal{L}$ over Σ and $P \times Q$ with $Q = \{e, o\}$. We will only*

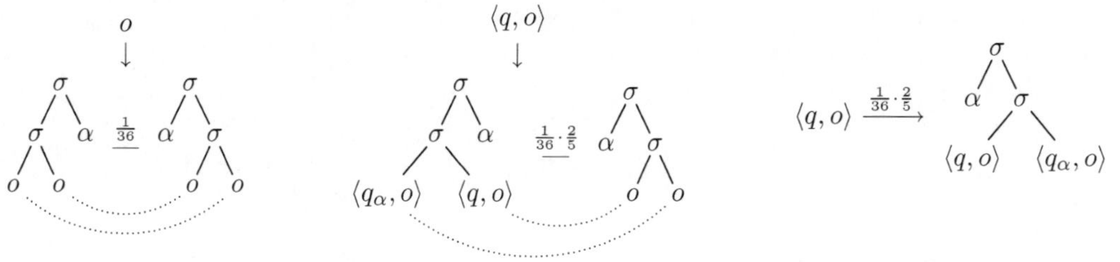

Figure 5: Illustration of the construction in the proof of Theorem 6 using the WRTG $\mathcal{K}$ of Example 7: some example rule (left), run of $\mathcal{K}$ on the input side of the rule (middle), and resulting rule (right).

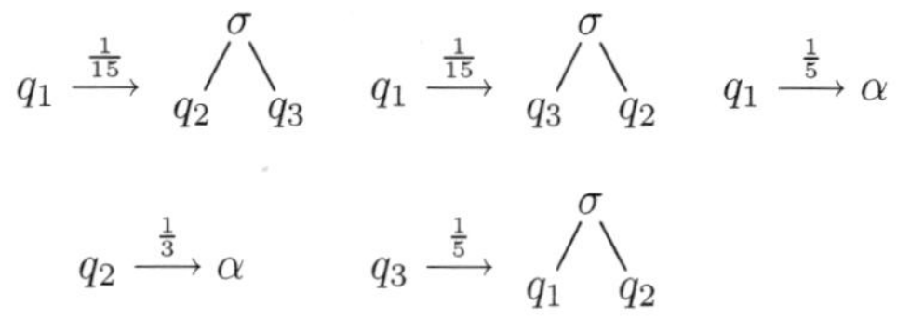

Figure 6: WRTG constructed in Example 7. We renamed the states and calculated the weights.

show rules of $\mathcal{L}$ that contribute to $\varphi_{\mathcal{L}}$. To the right of each rule we indicate from which state of $\mathcal{K}$ and which rule of $\mathcal{G}$ the rule was constructed.

$$\langle q_{\mathrm{S}}, o\rangle \xrightarrow{\frac{1}{6}\cdot\frac{2}{5}} \sigma(\langle q_\alpha, o\rangle, \langle p, e\rangle) \qquad q_{\mathrm{S}}, \rho_2$$

$$\langle q_{\mathrm{S}}, o\rangle \xrightarrow{\frac{1}{6}\cdot\frac{2}{5}} \sigma(\langle p, e\rangle, \langle q_\alpha, o\rangle) \qquad q_{\mathrm{S}}, \rho_3$$

$$\langle q_{\mathrm{S}}, o\rangle \xrightarrow{\frac{1}{3}\cdot\frac{3}{5}} \alpha \qquad q_{\mathrm{S}}, \rho_4$$

$$\langle q_\alpha, o\rangle \xrightarrow{\frac{1}{3}\cdot 1} \alpha \qquad q_\alpha, \rho_4$$

$$\langle p, e\rangle \xrightarrow{\frac{1}{2}\cdot\frac{2}{5}} \sigma(\langle q_{\mathrm{S}}, o\rangle, \langle q_\alpha, o\rangle) \qquad p, \rho_6$$

The initial state of $\mathcal{L}$ is $\langle q_{\mathrm{S}}, o\rangle$. It is easy to see that every $t \in T_\Sigma$ such that $\varphi_{\mathcal{L}}(t) \neq 0$ is thin, which means that $|\mathrm{pos}(t) \cap \mathbb{N}^n| \leq 2$ for every $n \in \mathbb{N}$.

7 Domain and range

Finally, let us consider the domain and range of a weighted tree transformation $\tau \colon T_\Sigma \times T_\Delta \to \mathbb{R}_{\geq 0}$. Again, we first give general definitions and deal with the infinite sums that might occur in them later. The *domain* $\mathrm{dom}(\tau)$ of τ and the *range* $\mathrm{range}(\tau)$ of τ are defined by

$$\big(\mathrm{dom}(\tau)\big)(s) = \sum_{u \in T_\Delta} \tau(s, u) \qquad (3)$$

$$\big(\mathrm{range}(\tau)\big)(t) = \sum_{u \in T_\Sigma} \tau(u, t) \qquad (4)$$

for every $s \in T_\Sigma$ and $t \in T_\Delta$. Obviously, the domain $\mathrm{dom}(\tau)$ is the range $\mathrm{range}(\tau^{-1})$ of the inverse of τ. Moreover, we can express the domain $\mathrm{dom}(\tau)$ of τ as the backward application $\tau^{-1}(\underline{1})$ where $\underline{1}$ is the weighted tree language that assigns the weight 1 to each tree. Note that $\underline{1}$ is recognizable for every ranked alphabet.

We note that the sums in Equations (3) and (4) might be infinite, but for input-productive (respectively, output-productive) STSG $\mathcal{G}$ the domain $\mathrm{dom}(\tau_{\mathcal{G}})$ (respectively, the range $\mathrm{range}(\tau_{\mathcal{G}})$) are well-defined by Proposition 5. Using those observations and Theorem 6 we can obtain the following statement.

Corollary 8. *Let $\mathcal{G}$ be an* STSG. *If $\mathcal{G}$ is input-productive, then $\mathrm{dom}(\tau_{\mathcal{G}})$ is recognizable. Moreover, if $\mathcal{G}$ is output-productive, then $\mathrm{range}(\tau_{\mathcal{G}})$ is recognizable.*

Proof. These statements follow directly from Theorem 6 with the help of the observation that $\mathrm{dom}(\tau_{\mathcal{G}}) = \tau_{\mathcal{G}}^{-1}(\underline{1})$ and $\mathrm{range}(\tau_{\mathcal{G}}) = \tau_{\mathcal{G}}(\underline{1})$. □

Conclusion

We showed that every output-productive STSG preserves recognizability under forward application. Dually, every input-productive STSG preserves recognizability under backward application. We presented direct and effective constructions for these operations. Special cases of those constructions can be used to compute the domain of an input-productive STSG and the range of an output-productive STSG. Finally, we presented a characterization of the power of STSG in terms of weighted bimorphisms.

Acknowledgements

ZOLTÁN FÜLÖP and HEIKO VOGLER were financially supported by the TÁMOP-4.2.2/08/1/2008-0008 program of the Hungarian National Development Agency. ANDREAS MALETTI was financially supported by the *Ministerio de Educación y Ciencia* (MEC) grant JDCI-2007-760.

References

Anne Abeillé, Yves Schabes, and Aravind K. Joshi. 1990. Using lexicalized TAGs for machine translation. In *Proc. 13th CoLing*, volume 3, pages 1–6. University of Helsinki, Finland.

Alfred V. Aho and Jeffrey D. Ullman. 1969. Translations on a context-free grammar. In *Proc. 1st STOC*, pages 93–112. ACM.

Athanasios Alexandrakis and Symeon Bozapalidis. 1987. Weighted grammars and Kleene's theorem. *Inf. Process. Lett.*, 24(1):1–4.

André Arnold and Max Dauchet. 1982. Morphismes et bimorphismes d'arbres. *Theoret. Comput. Sci.*, 20(1):33–93.

Joost Engelfriet, Eric Lilin, and Andreas Maletti. 2009. Extended multi bottom-up tree transducers — composition and decomposition. *Acta Inform.*, 46(8):561–590.

Zoltán Fülöp and Heiko Vogler. 2009. Weighted tree automata and tree transducers. In Manfred Droste, Werner Kuich, and Heiko Vogler, editors, *Handbook of Weighted Automata*, chapter 9, pages 313–403. Springer.

Michel Galley, Mark Hopkins, Kevin Knight, and Daniel Marcu. 2004. What's in a translation rule? In *Proc. HLT-NAACL 2004*, pages 273–280. ACL.

Ferenc Gécseg and Magnus Steinby. 1984. *Tree Automata*. Akadémiai Kiadó, Budapest, Hungary.

Ferenc Gécseg and Magnus Steinby. 1997. Tree languages. In Grzegorz Rozenberg and Arto Salomaa, editors, *Handbook of Formal Languages*, chapter 1, pages 1–68. Springer.

Jonathan S. Golan. 1999. *Semirings and their Applications*. Kluwer Academic.

Jonathan Graehl, Kevin Knight, and Jonathan May. 2008. Training tree transducers. *Computational Linguistics*, 34(3):391–427.

Udo Hebisch and Hanns J. Weinert. 1998. *Semirings — Algebraic Theory and Applications in Computer Science*. World Scientific.

Liang Huang and David Chiang. 2005. Better k-best parsing. In *Proc. 9th IWPT*, pages 53–64. ACL.

Kevin Knight and Jonathan Graehl. 2005. An overview of probabilistic tree transducers for natural language processing. In *Proc. 6th CICLing*, volume 3406 of LNCS, pages 1–24. Springer.

Philipp Koehn, Franz Josef Och, and Daniel Marcu. 2003. Statistical phrase-based translation. In *Proc. HLT-NAACL 2003*, pages 48–54. ACL.

Philip M. Lewis II and Richard Edwin Stearns. 1968. Syntax-directed transductions. *J. ACM*, 15(3):465–488.

Eric Lilin. 1981. Propriétés de clôture d'une extension de transducteurs d'arbres déterministes. In *Proc. 6th CAAP*, volume 112 of LNCS, pages 280–289. Springer.

Andreas Maletti, Jonathan Graehl, Mark Hopkins, and Kevin Knight. 2009. The power of extended top-down tree transducers. *SIAM J. Comput.*, 39(2):410–430.

Andreas Maletti. 2010. Why synchronous tree substitution grammars? In *Proc. HLT-NAACL 2010*. ACL. to appear.

David F. Martin and Steven A. Vere. 1970. On syntax-directed transduction and tree transducers. In *Proc. 2nd STOC*, pages 129–135. ACM.

Mark-Jan Nederhof and Giorgio Satta. 2006. Probabilistic parsing strategies. *J. ACM*, 53(3):406–436.

William C. Rounds. 1970. Mappings and grammars on trees. *Math. Systems Theory*, 4(3):257–287.

Yves Schabes. 1990. *Mathematical and computational aspects of lexicalized grammars*. Ph.D. thesis, University of Pennsylvania.

Stuart M. Shieber and Yves Schabes. 1990. Synchronous tree-adjoining grammars. In *Proc. 13th CoLing*, pages 253–258. ACL.

Stuart M. Shieber. 2004. Synchronous grammars as tree transducers. In *Proc. TAG+7*, pages 88–95. Simon Fraser University.

Stuart M. Shieber. 2006. Unifying synchronous tree adjoining grammars and tree transducers via bimorphisms. In *Proc. 11th EACL*, pages 377–384. ACL.

James W. Thatcher. 1970. Generalized^2 sequential machine maps. *J. Comput. System Sci.*, 4(4):339–367.

Kenji Yamada and Kevin Knight. 2001. A syntax-based statistical translation model. In *Proc. 39th ACL*, pages 523–530. ACL.

A Decoder for Probabilistic Synchronous Tree Insertion Grammars

Steve DeNeefe * **and Kevin Knight** *
USC Information Sciences Institute
4676 Admiralty Way
Marina del Rey, CA 90292, USA
{sdeneefe,knight}@isi.edu

Heiko Vogler †
Department of Computer Science
Technische Universität Dresden
D-01062 Dresden
Heiko.Vogler@tu-dresden.de

Abstract

Synchronous tree insertion grammars (STIG) are formal models for syntax-based machine translation. We formalize a decoder for probabilistic STIG; the decoder transforms every source-language string into a target-language tree and calculates the probability of this transformation.

1 Introduction

Tree adjoining grammars (TAG) were invented in (Joshi et al. 1975) in order to better characterize the string sets of natural languages[1]. One of TAG's important features is the ability to introduce two related syntactic units in a single rule, then push those two units arbitrarily far apart in subsequent derivation steps. For machine translation (MT) between two natural languages, each being generated by a TAG, the derivations of the two TAG may be synchronized (Abeille et al., 1990; Shieber and Shabes, 1990) in the spirit of syntax-directed transductions (Lewis and Stearns, 1968); this results in *synchronous TAG* (STAG). Recently, in (Nesson et al., 2005, 2006) probabilistic synchronous tree insertion grammars (pSTIG) were discussed as model of MT; a tree insertion grammar is a particular TAG in which the parsing problem is solvable in cubic-time (Schabes and Waters, 1994). In (DeNeefe, 2009; DeNeefe and Knight 2009) a decoder for pSTIG has been proposed which transforms source-language strings into (modifications of) derivation trees of the pSTIG. Nowadays, large-scale linguistic STAG rule bases are available.

In an independent tradition, the automata-theoretic investigation of the translation of trees led to the rich theory of tree transducers (Gécseg and Steinby, 1984, 1997). Roughly speaking, a tree transducer is a finite term rewriting system. If each rewrite rule carries a probablity or, in general, a weight from some semiring, then they are weighted tree transducers (Maletti, 2006, 2006a; Fülöp and Vogler, 2009). Such weighted tree transducers have also been used for the specification of MT of natural languages (Yamada and Knight, 2001; Knight and Graehl, 2005; Graehl et al., 2008; Knight and May 2009).

Martin and Vere (1970) and Schreiber (1975) established the first connections between the two traditions; also Shieber (2004, 2006) and Maletti (2008, 2010) investigated their relationship.

The problem addressed in this paper is the decoding of source-language strings into target-language trees where the transformation is described by a pSTIG. Currently, this decoding requires two steps: first, every source string is translated into a derivation tree of the underlying pSTIG (DeNeefe, 2009; DeNeefe and Knight 2009), and second, the derivation tree is transformed into the target tree using an embedded tree transducer (Shieber, 2006). We propose a transducer model, called a *bottom-up tree adjoining transducer*, which performs this decoding in a single step and, simultaneously, computes the probabilities of its derivations. As a basis of our approach, we present a formal definition of pSTIG.

2 Preliminaries

For two sets Σ and A, we let $U_\Sigma(A)$ be the set of all (unranked) trees over Σ in which also elements of A may label leaves. We abbreviate $U_\Sigma(\emptyset)$ by U_Σ. We denote the set of *positions*, *leaves*, and *non-leaves* of $\xi \in U_\Sigma$ by $\mathrm{pos}(\xi) \subseteq \mathbb{N}^*$, $\mathrm{lv}(\xi)$, and $\mathrm{nlv}(\xi)$, resp., where ε denotes the root of ξ and $w.i$ denotes the ith child of position w; $\mathrm{nlv}(\xi) = \mathrm{pos}(\xi) \setminus \mathrm{lv}(\xi)$. For a position $w \in \mathrm{pos}(\xi)$, the *label of* ξ *at* w (resp., *subtree of* ξ *at* w) is denoted

* financially supported by NSF STAGES project, grant #IIS-0908532.

† financially supported by DFG VO 1011/5-1.

[1] see (Joshi and Shabes, 1997) for a survey

Proceedings of the 2010 Workshop on Applications of Tree Automata in Natural Language Processing, ACL 2010, pages 10–18, Uppsala, Sweden, 16 July 2010.

by $\xi(w)$ (resp., $\xi|_w$). If additionally $\zeta \in U_\Sigma(A)$, then $\xi[\zeta]_w$ denotes the tree which is obtained from ξ by replacing its subtree at w by ζ. For every $\Delta \subseteq \Sigma \cup A$, the set $\text{pos}_\Delta(\xi)$ is the set of all those positions $w \in \text{pos}(\xi)$ such that $\xi(w) \in \Delta$. Similarly, we can define $\text{lv}_\Delta(\xi)$ and $\text{nlv}_\Delta(\xi)$. The *yield of* ξ is the sequence $\text{yield}(\xi) \in (\Sigma \cup A)^*$ of symbols that label the leaves from left to right.

If we associate with $\sigma \in \Sigma$ a rank $k \in \mathbb{N}$, then we require that in every tree $\xi \in U_\Sigma(A)$ every σ-labeled position has exactly k children.

3 Probabilistic STAG and STIG

First we will define probabilistic STAG, and second, as a special case, probabilistic STIG.

Let N and T be two disjoint sets of, resp., nonterminals and terminals. A *substitution rule* r is a tuple $(\zeta_s, \zeta_t, V, W, P^r_{\text{adj}})$ where

- $\zeta_s, \zeta_t \in U_N(T)$ (*source* and *target tree*) and $|\text{lv}_N(\zeta_s)| = |\text{lv}_N(\zeta_t)|$,
- $V \subseteq \text{lv}_N(\zeta_s) \times \text{lv}_N(\zeta_t)$ (*substitution sites*), V is a one-to-one relation, and $|V| = |\text{lv}_N(\zeta_s)|$,
- $W \subseteq \text{nlv}_N(\zeta_s) \times \text{nlv}_N(\zeta_t)$ (*potential adjoining sites*), and
- $P^r_{\text{adj}} : W \to [0, 1]$ (*adjoining probability*).

An *auxiliary rule* r is a tuple $(\zeta_s, \zeta_t, V, W, *, P^r_{\text{adj}})$ where ζ_s, ζ_t, W, and P^r_{adj} are defined as above and

- V is defined as above except that $|V| = |\text{lv}_N(\zeta_s)| - 1$ and
- $* = (*_s, *_t) \in \text{lv}_N(\zeta_s) \times \text{lv}_N(\zeta_t)$ and neither $*_s$ nor $*_t$ occurs in any element of V; moreover, $\zeta_s(\varepsilon) = \zeta_s(*_s)$ and $\zeta_t(\varepsilon) = \zeta_t(*_t)$, and $*_s \neq \varepsilon \neq *_t$; the node $*_s$ (and $*_t$) is called the *foot-node of* ζ_s (resp., ζ_t).

An *(elementary) rule* is either a substitution rule or an auxiliary rule. The *root-category* of a rule r is the tuple $(\zeta_s(\varepsilon), \zeta_t(\varepsilon))$, denoted by $\text{rc}(r)$.

A *probabilistic synchronous tree adjoining grammar* (pSTAG) is a tuple $G = (N, T, (S_s, S_t), \mathcal{S}, \mathcal{A}, P)$ such that N and T are two disjoint sets (resp., of nonterminals and terminals), $(S_s, S_t) \in N \times N$ (*start nonterminal*), $\mathcal{S}$ and $\mathcal{A}$ are finite sets of, resp., substitution rules and auxiliary rules, and $P : \mathcal{S} \cup \mathcal{A} \to [0, 1]$ such that for every $(A, B) \in N \times N$,

$$\sum_{\substack{r \in \mathcal{S} \\ \text{rc}(r)=(A,B)}} P(r) = 1 \quad \text{and} \quad \sum_{\substack{r \in \mathcal{A} \\ \text{rc}(r)=(A,B)}} P(r) = 1$$

assuming that in each case the number of summands is not zero. In the following, let G always denote an arbitrary pSTAG.

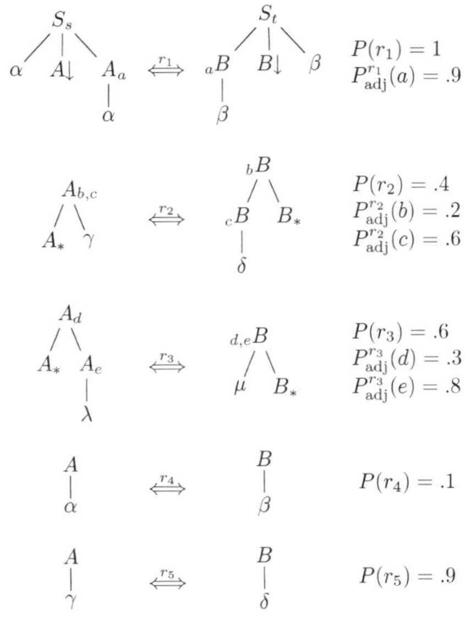

Figure 1: The running example pSTAG G.

In Fig. 1 we show the rules of our running example pSTAG, where the capital Roman letters are the nonterminals and the small Greek letters are the terminals. The substitution site (in rule r_1) is indicated by $\downarrow$, and the potential adjoining sites are denoted[2] by a, b, c, d, and e. For instance, in formal notation the rules r_1 and r_2 are written as follows:

$$r_1 = (S_s(\alpha, A, A(\alpha)),\ S_t(B(\beta), B, \beta),\ \{\downarrow\}, \{a\}, P^{r_1}_{\text{adj}})$$

where $\downarrow = (2, 2)$ and $a = (3, 1)$, and

$$r_2 = (A(A, \gamma),\ B(B(\delta), B),\ \emptyset,\ \{b, c\}, *, P^{r_2}_{\text{adj}})$$

where $b = (\varepsilon, \varepsilon)$, $c = (\varepsilon, 1)$, and $* = (1, 2)$.

In the derivation relation of G we will distinguish four types of steps:

1. substitution of a rule at a substitution site (substitution),
2. deciding to turn a potential adjoining site into an activated adjoining site (activation),
3. deciding to drop a potential adjoining site, i.e., not to adjoin, (non-adjoining) and
4. adjoining of a rule at an activated adjoining site (adjoining).

In the sentential forms (defined below) we will maintain for every adjoining site w a two-valued flag $g(w)$ indicating whether w is a potential ($g(w) = \text{p}$) or an activated site ($g(w) = \text{a}$).

The *set of sentential forms of* G is the set $\text{SF}(G)$ of all tuples $\kappa = (\xi_s, \xi_t, V, W, g)$ with

[2] Their placement (as left or right index) does not play a role yet, but will later when we introduce pSTIG.

- $\xi_s, \xi_t \in U_N(T)$,
- $V \subseteq \mathrm{lv}_N(\xi_s) \times \mathrm{lv}_N(\xi_t)$ is a one-to-one relation, $|V| = |\mathrm{lv}_N(\xi_s)| = |\mathrm{lv}_N(\xi_t)|$,
- $W \subseteq \mathrm{nlv}_N(\xi_s) \times \mathrm{nlv}_N(\xi_t)$, and
- $g : W \to \{\mathrm{p}, \mathrm{a}\}$.

The *derivation relation (of G)* is the binary relation $\Rightarrow \; \subseteq \; \mathrm{SF}(G) \times \mathrm{SF}(G)$ such that for every $\kappa_1 = (\xi_s^1, \xi_t^1, V_1, W_1, g_1)$ and $\kappa_2 = (\xi_s^2, \xi_t^2, V_2, W_2, g_2)$ we have $\kappa_1 \Rightarrow \kappa_2$ iff one of the following is true:

1. (substitution) there are $w = (w_s, w_t) \in V_1$ and $r = (\zeta_s, \zeta_t, V, W, P^r_{\mathrm{adj}}) \in \mathcal{S}$ such that
   - $(\xi_s^1(w_s), \xi_t^1(w_t)) = \mathrm{rc}(r)$,
   - $\xi_s^2 = \xi_s^1[\zeta_s]_{w_s}$ and $\xi_t^2 = \xi_t^1[\zeta_t]_{w_t}$,
   - $V_2 = (V_1 \setminus \{w\}) \cup w.V$,[3]
   - $W_2 = W_1 \cup w.W$, and
   - g_2 is the union of g_1 and the set of pairs $(w.u, \mathrm{p})$ for every $u \in W$;

   this step is denoted by $\kappa_1 \overset{w,r}{\Longrightarrow} \kappa_2$;

2. (activation) there is a $w \in W_1$ with $g_1(w) = \mathrm{p}$ and $(\xi_s^1, \xi_t^1, V_1, W_1) = (\xi_s^2, \xi_t^2, V_2, W_2)$, and g_2 is the same as g_1 except that $g_2(w) = \mathrm{a}$; this step is denoted by $\kappa_1 \overset{w}{\Longrightarrow} \kappa_2$;

3. (non-adjoining) there is $w \in W_1$ with $g_1(w) = \mathrm{p}$ and $(\xi_s^1, \xi_t^1, V_1) = (\xi_s^2, \xi_t^2, V_2)$, $W_2 = W_1 \setminus \{w\}$, and g_2 is g_1 restricted to W_2; this step is denoted by $\kappa_1 \overset{\neg w}{\Longrightarrow} \kappa_2$;

4. (adjoining) there are $w \in W_1$ with $g_1(w) = \mathrm{a}$, and $r = (\zeta_s, \zeta_t, V, W, *, P^r_{\mathrm{adj}}) \in \mathcal{A}$ such that, for $w = (w_s, w_t)$,
   - $(\xi_s^1(w_s), \xi_t^1(w_t)) = \mathrm{rc}(r)$,
   - $\xi_s^2 = \xi_s^1[\zeta_s']_{w_s}$ where $\zeta_s' = \zeta_s[\xi_s^1|_{w_s}]_{*_s}$, $\xi_t^2 = \xi_t^1[\zeta_t']_{w_t}$ where $\zeta_t' = \zeta_t[\xi_t^1|_{w_t}]_{*_t}$,
   - V_2 is the smallest set such that (i) for every $(u_s, u_t) \in V_1$ we have $(u_s', u_t') \in V_2$ where

   $$u_s' = \begin{cases} u_s & \text{if } w_s \text{ is not a prefix of } u_s, \\ w_s.*_s.u & \text{if } u_s = w_s.u \text{ for some } u; \end{cases}$$

     and u_t' is obtained in the same way from u_t, w_t, and $*_t$, and (ii) V_2 contains $w.V$;
   - W_2 is the smallest set such that (i) for every $(u_s, u_t) \in W_1 \setminus \{w\}$ we have $(u_s', u_t') \in W_2$ where u_s' and u_t' are obtained in the same way as for V_2, and $g_2(u_s', u_t') = g_1(u_s, u_t)$ and (ii) W_2 contains $w.W$ and $g_2(w.u) = \mathrm{p}$ for every $u \in W$;

   this step is denoted by $\kappa_1 \overset{w,r}{\Longrightarrow} \kappa_2$.

[3] $w.V = \{(w_s.v_s, w_t.v_t) \mid (v_s, v_t) \in V\}$

In Fig. 2 we show a derivation of our running example pSTAG where activated adjoining sites are indicated by surrounding circles, the other adjoining sites are potential.

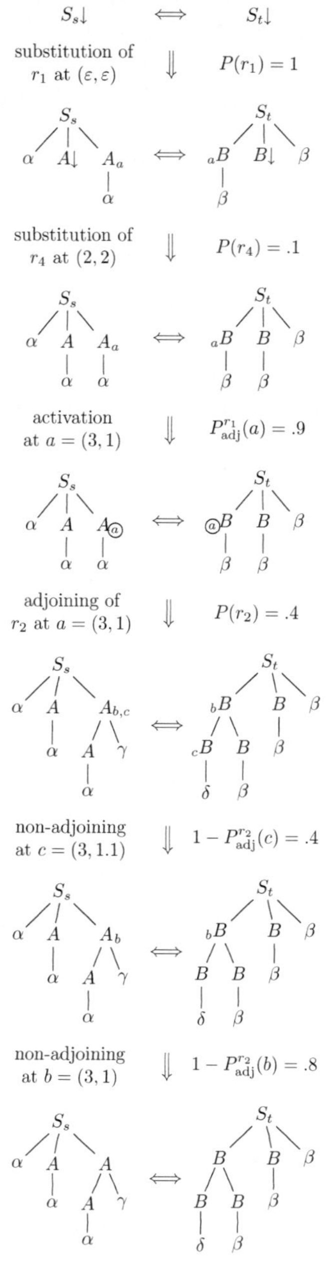

Figure 2: An example derivation with total probability $1 \times .1 \times .9 \times .4 \times .4 \times .8 = .01152$.

The only *initial* sentential form is $\kappa_{\mathrm{in}} = (S_s, S_t, \{(\varepsilon,\varepsilon)\}, \emptyset, \emptyset)$. A sentential form κ is *final* if it has the form $(\xi_s, \xi_t, \emptyset, \emptyset, \emptyset)$. Let $\kappa \in \mathrm{SF}(G)$. A *derivation (of κ)* is a sequence d of the form $\kappa_0 u_1 \kappa_1 \ldots u_n \kappa_n$ with $\kappa_0 = \kappa_{\mathrm{in}}$ and $n \geq 0$, $\kappa_{i-1} \overset{u_i}{\Rightarrow} \kappa_i$ for every $1 \leq i \leq n$ (and $\kappa_n = \kappa$). We denote κ_n also by $\text{last}(d)$, and the set of all derivations of κ (resp., derivations) by $D(\kappa)$ (resp., D). We call $d \in D$ *successful* if $\text{last}(d)$ is final.

The *tree transformation computed by* G is the relation $\tau_G \subseteq U_N(T) \times U_N(T)$ with $(\xi_s, \xi_t) \in \tau_G$ iff there is a successful derivation of $(\xi_s, \xi_t, \emptyset, \emptyset, \emptyset)$.

Our definition of the probability of a derivation is based on the following observation.[4] Let $d \in D(\kappa)$ for some $\kappa = (\xi_s, \xi_t, V, W, g)$. Then, for every $w \in W$, the rule which created w and the corresponding local position in that rule can be retrieved from d. Let us denote this rule by $r(d, \kappa, w)$ and the local position by $l(d, \kappa, w)$.

Now let d be the derivation $\kappa_0 u_1 \kappa_1 \dots u_n \kappa_n$. Then the *probability of* d is defined by

$$P(d) = \prod_{1 \leq i \leq n} P_d(\kappa_{i-1} \overset{u_i}{\Rightarrow} \kappa_i)$$

where

1. (substitution) $P_d(\kappa_{i-1} \overset{w,r}{\Longrightarrow} \kappa_i) = P(r)$
2. (activation) $P_d(\kappa_{i-1} \overset{w}{\Longrightarrow} \kappa_i) = P^{r'}_{\text{adj}}(w')$ where $r' = r(d, \kappa_{i-1}, w)$ and $w' = l(d, \kappa_{i-1}, w)$
3. (non-adjoining) $P_d(\kappa_{i-1} \overset{\neg w}{\Longrightarrow} \kappa_i) = 1 - P^{r'}_{\text{adj}}(w')$ where r' and w' are defined as in the activation case
4. (adjoining) $P_d(\kappa_{i-1} \overset{w,r}{\Longrightarrow} \kappa_i) = P(r)$.

In order to describe the generative model of G, we impose a deterministic strategy sel on the derivation relation in order to obtain, for every sentential form, a probability distribution among the follow-up sentential forms. A *deterministic derivation strategy* is a mapping $\text{sel} : \text{SF}(G) \to (\mathbb{N}^* \times \mathbb{N}^*) \cup \{\bot\}$ such that for every $\kappa = (\xi_s, \xi_t, V, W, g) \in \text{SF}(G)$, we have that $\text{sel}(\kappa) \in V \cup W$ if $V \cup W \neq \emptyset$, and $\text{sel}(\kappa) = \bot$ otherwise. In other words, sel chooses the next site to operate on. Then we define $\Rightarrow_{\text{sel}}$ in the same way as $\Rightarrow$ but in each of the cases we require that $w = \text{sel}(\kappa_1)$. Moreover, for every derivation $d \in D$, we denote by $\text{next}(d)$ the set of all derivations of the form $du\kappa$ where $\text{last}(d) \overset{u}{\Rightarrow}_{\text{sel}} \kappa$.

The generative model of G comprises all the generative stories of G. A *generative story* is a tree $t \in U_D$; the root of t is labeled by κ_{in}. Let $w \in \text{pos}(t)$ and $t(w) = d$. Then either w is a leaf, because we have stopped the generative story at w, or w has $|\text{next}(d)|$ children, each one represents exactly one possible decision about how to extend d by a single derivation step (where their order does not matter). Then, for every generative story t, we have that

$$\sum_{w \in \text{lv}(t)} P(t(w)) = 1 \ .$$

We note that (D, next, μ) can be considered as a discrete Markov chain (cf., e.g. (Baier et al., 2009)) where the initial probability distribution $\mu : D \to [0, 1]$ maps $d = \kappa_{\text{in}}$ to 1, and all the other derivations to 0.

A *probabilistic synchronous tree insertion grammar* (pSTIG) G is a pSTAG except that for every rule $r = (\zeta_s, \zeta_t, V, W, P^r_{\text{adj}})$ or $r = (\zeta_s, \zeta_t, V, W, *, P^r_{\text{adj}})$ we have that

- if $r \in \mathcal{A}$, then $|\text{lv}(\zeta_s)| \geq 2$ and $|\text{lv}(\zeta_t)| \geq 2$,
- for $* = (*_s, *_t)$ we have that $*_s$ is either the rightmost leaf of ζ_s or its leftmost one; then we call r, resp., *L-auxiliary in the source* and *R-auxiliary in the source*; similarly, we restrict $*_t$; the *source-spine of* r (*target-spine of* r) is the set of prefixes of $*_s$ (resp., of $*_t$)
- $W \subseteq \text{nlv}_N(\zeta_s) \times \{\text{L}, \text{R}\} \times \text{nlv}_N(\zeta_t) \times \{\text{L}, \text{R}\}$ where the new components are the *direction-type* of the potential adjoining site, and
- for every $(w_s, \delta_s, w_t, \delta_t) \in W$, if w_s lies on the source-spine of r and r is L-auxiliary (R-auxiliary) in the source, then $\delta_s = \text{L}$ (resp., $\delta_s = \text{R}$), and corresponding restrictions hold for the target component.

According to the four possibilities for the foot-node $*$ we call r LL-, LR-, RL-, or RR-auxiliary. The restriction for the probability distribution P of G is modified such that for every $(A, B) \in N \times N$ and $x, y \in \{\text{L}, \text{R}\}$:

$$\sum_{\substack{r \in \mathcal{A},\ \text{rc}(r) = (A,B) \\ r \text{ is } xy-\text{auxiliary}}} P(r) = 1 \ .$$

In the derivation relation of the pSTIG G we will have to make sure that the direction-type of the chosen adjoining site w matches with the type of auxiliarity of the auxiliary rule. Again we assume that the data structure $\text{SF}(G)$ is enriched such that for every potential adjoining site w of $\kappa \in \text{SF}(G)$ we know its direction-type $\text{dir}(w)$.

We define the derivation relation of the pSTIG G to be the binary relation $\Rightarrow_I \subseteq \text{SF}(G) \times \text{SF}(G)$ such that we have $\kappa_1 \Rightarrow_I \kappa_2$ iff (i) $\kappa_1 \Rightarrow \kappa_2$ and

[4] We note that a different definition occurs in (Nesson et al., 2005, 2006).

(ii) if adjoining takes place at w, then the used auxiliary rule must be $\mathrm{dir}(w)$-auxiliary. Since $\Rightarrow_I$ is a subset of $\Rightarrow$, the concepts of derivation, successful derivation, and tree transformation are defined also for a pSTIG.

In fact, our running example pSTAG in Fig. 1 is a pSTIG, where r_2 and r_3 are RL-auxiliary and every potential adjoining site has direction-type RL; the derivation shown in Fig. 2 is a pSTIG-derivation.

4 Bottom-up tree adjoining transducer

Here we introduce the concept of a bottom-up tree adjoining transducer (BUTAT) which will be used to formalize a decoder for a pSTIG.

A BUTAT is a finite-state machine which translates strings into trees. The left-hand side of each rule is a string over terminal symbols and state-variable combinations. A variable is either a substitution variable or an adjoining variable; a substitution variable (resp., adjoining variable) can have an output tree (resp., output tree with foot node) as value. Intuitively, each variable value is a translation of the string that has been reduced to the corresponding state. The right-hand side of a rule has the form $q(\zeta)$ where q is a state and ζ is an output tree (with or without foot-node); ζ may contain the variables from the left-hand side of the rule. Each rule has a probability $p \in [0,1]$.

In fact, BUTAT can be viewed as the string-to-tree version of bottom-up tree transducers (Engelfriet, 1975; Gecseg and Steinby, 1984,1997) in which, in addition to substitution, adjoining is allowed.

Formally, we let $X = \{x_1, x_2, \ldots\}$ and $F = \{f_1, f_2, \ldots\}$ be the sets of *substitution variables* and *adjoining variables*, resp. Each substitution variable (resp., adjoining variable) has rank 0 (resp., 1). Thus when used in a tree, substitution variables are leaves, while adjoining variables have a single child.

A *bottom-up tree adjoining transducer* (BUTAT) is a tuple $M = (Q, \Gamma, \Delta, Q_f, R)$ where

- Q is a finite set (of *states*),
- Γ is an alphabet (of *input symbols*), assuming that $Q \cap \Gamma = \emptyset$,
- Δ is an alphabet (of *output symbols*),
- $Q_f \subseteq Q$ (set of *final states*), and
- R is a finite set of rules of the form

$$\gamma_0\, q_1(z_1)\, \gamma_1 \,\ldots\, q_k(z_k)\, \gamma_k \xrightarrow{p} q(\zeta) \quad (\dagger)$$

where $p \in [0,1]$ (*probability* of $(\dagger)$), $k \geq 0$, $\gamma_0, \gamma_1, \ldots, \gamma_k \in \Gamma^*$, $q, q_1, \ldots, q_k \in Q$, $z_1, \ldots, z_k \in X \cup F$, and $\zeta \in \mathrm{RHS}(k)$ where $\mathrm{RHS}(k)$ is the set of all trees over $\Delta \cup \{z_1, \ldots, z_k\} \cup \{*\}$ in which the nullary $*$ occurs at most once.

The set of *intermediate results of* M is the set $\mathrm{IR}(M) = \{\iota \mid \iota \in U_\Delta(\{*\}), |\mathrm{pos}_{\{*\}}(\iota)| \leq 1\}$ and the set of *sentential forms of* M is the set $\mathrm{SF}(M) = (\Gamma \cup \{q(\iota) \mid q \in Q, \iota \in \mathrm{IR}(M)\})^*$. The *derivation relation induced by* M is the binary relation $\Rightarrow \subseteq \mathrm{SF}(M) \times \mathrm{SF}(M)$ such that for every $\xi_1, \xi_2 \in \mathrm{SF}(M)$ we define $\xi_1 \Rightarrow \xi_2$ iff there are $\xi, \xi' \in \mathrm{SF}(M)$, there is a rule of the form $(\dagger)$ in R, and there are $\zeta_1, \ldots, \zeta_k \in \mathrm{IR}(M)$ such that:

- for every $1 \leq i \leq k$: if $z_i \in X$, then ζ_i does not contain $*$; if $z_i \in F$, then ζ_i contains $*$ exactly once,
- $\xi_1 = \xi\, \gamma_0\, q_1(\zeta_1)\, \gamma_1 \,\ldots\, q_k(\zeta_k)\, \gamma_k\, \xi'$, and
- $\xi_2 = \xi\, q(\theta(\zeta))\, \xi'$

where θ is a function that replaces variables in a right-hand side with their values (subtrees) from the left-hand side of the rule. Formally, $\theta : \mathrm{RHS}(k) \rightarrow \mathrm{IR}(M)$ is defined as follows:

(i) for every $\xi = \delta(\xi_1, \ldots, \xi_n) \in \mathrm{RHS}(k)$, $\delta \in \Delta$, we have $\theta(\xi) = \delta(\theta(\xi_1), \ldots, \theta(\xi_n))$,

(ii) (substitution) for every $z_i \in X$, we have $\theta(z_i) = \zeta_i$,

(iii) (adjoining) for every $z_i \in F$ and $\xi \in \mathrm{RHS}(k)$, we have $\theta(z_i(\xi)) = \zeta_i[\theta(\xi)]_v$ where v is the uniquely determined position of $*$ in ζ_i, and

(iv) $\theta(*) = *$.

Clearly, the probablity of a rule carries over to derivation steps that employ this rule. Since, as usual, a derivation d is a sequence of derivation steps, we let the *probability of* d be the product of the probabilities of its steps.

The *string-to-tree transformation computed by* M is the set τ_M of all tuples $(\gamma, \xi) \in \Gamma^* \times U_\Delta$ such that there is a derivation of the form $\gamma \Rightarrow^* q(\xi)$ for some $q \in Q_f$.

5 Decoder for pSTIG

Now we construct the decoder $\mathrm{dec}(G)$ for a pSTIG G that transforms source strings directly into target trees and simultaneously computes the probability of the corresponding derivation of G. This decoder is formalized as a BUTAT.

Since $\mathrm{dec}(G)$ is a string-to-tree transducer, we

have to transform the source tree ζ_s of a rule r into a left-hand side ρ of a $\mathrm{dec}(G)$-rule. This is done similarly to (DeNeefe and Knight, 2009) by traversing ζ_s via recursive descent using a mapping φ (see an example after Theorem 1); this creates appropriate state-variable combinations for all substitution sites and potential adjoining sites of r. In particular, the source component of the direction-type of a potential adjoining site determines the position of the corresponding combination in ρ. If there are several potential adjoining sites with the same source component, then we create a ρ for every permutation of these sites. The right-hand side of a $\mathrm{dec}(G)$-rule is obtained by traversing the target tree ζ_t via recursive descent using a mapping ψ_ρ and, whenever a nonterminal with a potential adjoining site w is met, a new position labeled by f_w is inserted.[5] If there is more than one potential adjoining site, then the set of all those sites is ordered as in the left-hand side ρ from top to bottom.

Apart from these main rules we will employ rules which implement the decision of whether or not to turn a potential adjoining site w into an activated adjoining site. Rules for the first purpose just pass the already computed output tree through from left to right, whereas rules for the second purpose create for an empty left-hand side the output tree $*$.

We will use the state behavior of $\mathrm{dec}(G)$ in order to check that (i) the nonterminals of a substitution or potential adjoining site match the root-category of the used rule, (ii) the direction-type of an adjoining site matches the auxiliarity of the chosen auxiliary rule, and (iii) the decisions of whether or not to adjoin for each rule r of G are kept separate.

Whereas each pair (ξ_s, ξ_t) in the translation of G is computed in a top-down way, starting at the initial sentential form and substituting and adjoining to the present sentential form, $\mathrm{dec}(G)$ builds ξ_t in a bottom-up way. This change of direction is legitimate, because adjoining is associative (Vijay-Shanker and Weir, 1994), i.e., it leads to the same result whether we first adjoin r_2 to r_1, and then align r_3 to the resulting tree, or first adjoin r_3 to r_2, and then adjoin the resulting tree to r_1.

In Fig. 3 we show some rules of the decoder of our running example pSTIG and in Fig. 4 the derivation of this decoder which correponds to the derivation in Fig. 2.

Theorem 1. Let G be a pSTIG over N and T. Then there is a BUTAT $\mathrm{dec}(G)$ such that for every $(\xi_s, \xi_t) \in U_N(T) \times U_N(T)$ and $p \in [0, 1]$ the following two statements are equivalent:

1. there is a successful derivation of $(\xi_s, \xi_t, \emptyset, \emptyset, \emptyset)$ by G with probability p,
2. there is a derivation from $\mathrm{yield}(\xi_s)$ to $[S_s, S_t](\xi_t)$ by $\mathrm{dec}(G)$ with probability p.

PROOF. Let $G = (N, T, [S_s, S_t], \mathcal{S}, \mathcal{A}, P)$ be a pSTIG. We will construct the BUTAT $\mathrm{dec}(G) = (Q, T, N \cup T, \{[S_s, S_t]\}, R)$ as follows (where the mappings φ and ψ_ρ will be defined below):

- $Q = [N \times N] \cup [N \times \{\mathrm{L}, \mathrm{R}\} \times N \times \{\mathrm{L}, \mathrm{R}\}] \cup \{[r, w] \mid r \in \mathcal{A}, w \text{ is an adjoining site of } r\}$,
- R is the smallest set R' of rules such that for every $r \in \mathcal{S} \cup \mathcal{A}$ of the form $(\zeta_s, \zeta_t, V, W, P^r_{\mathrm{adj}})$ or $(\zeta_s, \zeta_t, V, W, *, P^r_{\mathrm{adj}})$:
  - for every $\rho \in \varphi(\varepsilon)$, if $r \in \mathcal{S}$, then the main rule

$$\rho \xrightarrow{P(r)} [\zeta_s(\varepsilon), \zeta_t(\varepsilon)]\big(\psi_\rho(\varepsilon)\big)$$

    is in R', and if $r \in \mathcal{A}$ and r is $\delta_s\delta_t$-auxiliary, then the main rule

$$\rho \xrightarrow{P(r)} [\zeta_s(\varepsilon), \delta_s, \zeta_t(\varepsilon), \delta_t]\big(\psi_\rho(\varepsilon)\big)$$

    is in R', and
  - for every $w = (w_s, \delta_s, w_t, \delta_t) \in W$ the rules

$$q_w\big(f_w\big) \xrightarrow{P^r_{\mathrm{adj}}(w)} [r, w]\big(f_w(*)\big)$$

    with $q_w = [\zeta(w_s), \delta_s, \zeta_t(w_t), \delta_t]$ for activation at w, and the rule

$$\varepsilon \xrightarrow{1 - P^r_{\mathrm{adj}}(w)} [r, w](*)$$

    for non-adjoining at w are in R'.

We define the mapping

$$\varphi : \mathrm{pos}(\zeta_s) \to \mathcal{P}((T \cup Q(X \cup F))^*)$$

with $Q(X \cup F) = \{q(z) \mid q \in Q, z \in X \cup F\}$ inductively on its argument as follows. Let $w \in \mathrm{pos}(\zeta_s)$ and let w have n children.

(a) Let $\zeta_s(w) \in T$. Then $\varphi(w) = \{\zeta_s(w)\}$.

[5] We will allow variables to have structured indices that are not elements of $\mathbb{N}$. However, by applying a bijective renaming, we can always obtain rules of the form (†).

(b) (substitution site) Let $\zeta_s(w) \in N$ and let $w' \in \text{pos}(\zeta_t)$ such that $(w, w') \in V$. Then

$$\varphi(w) = \{[\zeta_s(w), \zeta_t(w')](x_{(w,w')})\}.$$

(c) (adjoining site) Let $\zeta_s(w) \in N$ and let there be an adjoining site in W with w as first component. Then, we define $\varphi(w)$ to be the smallest set such that for every permutation $(u_1, \ldots, u_l)$ (resp., $(v_1, \ldots, v_m)$) of all the L-adjoining (resp., R-adjoining) sites in W with w as first component, the set[6]

$$J \circ \varphi(w.1) \circ \ldots \circ \varphi(w.n) \circ K$$

is a subset of $\varphi(w)$, where $J = \{u'_1 \ldots u'_l\}$ and $K = \{v'_m \ldots v'_1\}$ and

$$u'_i = [r, u_i](f_{u_i}) \text{ and } v'_j = [r, v_j](f_{v_j})$$

for $1 \leq i \leq l$ and $1 \leq j \leq m$.

(d) Let $\zeta_s(w) \in N$, $w \neq *$, and let w be neither the first component of a substitution site in V nor the first component of an adjoining site in W. Then

$$\varphi(w) = \varphi(w.1) \circ \ldots \circ \varphi(w.n) \ .$$

(e) Let $w = *$. Then we define $\varphi(w) = \{\varepsilon\}$.

For every $\rho \in \varphi(\varepsilon)$, we define the mapping

$$\psi_\rho : \text{pos}(\zeta_t) \to U_{N \cup F \cup X}(T \cup \{*\})$$

inductively on its argument as follows. Let $w \in \text{pos}(\zeta_t)$ and let w have n children.

(a) Let $\zeta_t(w) \in T$. Then $\psi_\rho(w) = \zeta_t(w)$.

(b) (substitution site) Let $\zeta_t(w) \in N$ and let $w' \in \text{pos}(\zeta_s)$ such that $(w', w) \in V$. Then $\psi_\rho(w) = x_{(w',w)}$.

(c) (adjoining site) Let $\zeta_t(w) \in N$ and let there be an adjoining site in W with w as third component. Then let $\{u_1, \ldots, u_l\} \subseteq W$ be the set of all potential adjoining sites with w as third component, and we define

$$\psi_\rho(w) = f_{u_1}(\ldots f_{u_l}(\zeta) \ldots)$$

where $\zeta = \zeta_t(w)(\psi_\rho(w.1), \ldots, \psi_\rho(w.n))$ and the u_i's occur in $\psi_\rho(w)$ (from the root towards the leaves) in exactly the same order as they occur in ρ (from left to right).

(d) Let $\zeta_t(w) \in N$, $w \neq *$, and let w be neither the second component of a substitution site in V nor the third component of an adjoining site in W. Then

$$\psi_\rho(w) = \zeta_t(w)(\psi_\rho(w.1), \ldots, \psi_\rho(w.n)).$$

(e) Let $w = *$. Then $\psi_\rho(w) = *$.

With $\text{dec}(G)$ constructed as shown, for each derivation of G there is a corresponding derivation of $\text{dec}(G)$, with the same probability, and vice versa. The derivations proceed in opposite directions. Each sentential form in one has an equivalent sentential form in the other, and each step of the derivations correspond. There is no space to present the full proof, but let us give a slightly more precise idea about the formal relationship between the derivations of G and $\text{dec}(G)$.

In the usual way we can associate a derivation tree d^t with every successful derivation d of G. Assume that $\text{last}(d) = (\xi_s, \xi_t, \emptyset, \emptyset, \emptyset)$, and let E_s and E_t be the embedded tree transducers (Shieber, 2006) associated with, respectively, the source component and the target component of G. Then it was shown in (Shieber, 2006) that $\tau_{E_s}(d^t) = \xi_s$ and $\tau_{E_t}(d^t) = \xi_t$ where τ_E denotes the tree-to-tree transduction computed by an embedded tree transducer E. Roughly speaking, E_s and E_t reproduce the derivations of, respectively, the source component and the target component of G that are prescribed by d^t. Thus, for $\kappa = (\xi'_s, \xi'_t, V, W, g)$, if $\kappa_{in} \Rightarrow^*_G \kappa$ and κ is a prefix of d, then there is exactly one subtree $d^t[(w, w')]$ of d^t associated with every $(w, w') \in V \cup W$, which prescribes how to continue at (w, w') with the reproduction of d. Having this in mind, we obtain the sentential form of the $\text{dec}(G)$-derivation which corresponds to κ by applying a modification of φ to κ where the modification amounts to replacing $x_{(w,w')}$ and $f_{(w,w')}$ by $\tau_{E_t}(d^t[(w, w')])$; note that $\tau_{E_t}(d^t[(w, w')])$ might contain $*$. ■

As illustration of the construction in Theorem 1 let us apply the mappings φ and ψ_ρ to rule r_2 of Fig. 1, i.e., to $r_2 = (\zeta_s, \zeta_t, \emptyset, \{b, c\}, *, P^{r_2}_{\text{adj}})$ with $\zeta_s = A(A, \gamma)$, $\zeta_t = B(B(\delta), B)$, $b = (\varepsilon, \text{R}, \varepsilon, \text{L})$, $c = (\varepsilon, \text{R}, 1, \text{L})$, and $* = (1, 2)$.

Let us calculate $\varphi(\varepsilon)$ on ζ_s. Due to (c),

$$\varphi(\varepsilon) = J \circ \varphi(1) \circ \varphi(2) \circ K.$$

Since there are no L-adjoinings at ε, we have that $J = \{\varepsilon\}$. Since there are the R-adjoinings b and c at ε, we have the two permutations (b, c) and (c, b).

$(v_1, v_2) = (b, c)$: $K = \{[r_2, c](f_c)[r_2, b](f_b)\}$

$(v_1, v_2) = (c, b)$: $K = \{[r_2, b](f_b)[r_2, c](f_c)\}$

Due to (e) and (a), we have that $\varphi(1) = \{\varepsilon\}$ and $\varphi(2) = \{\gamma\}$, resp. Thus, $\varphi(\varepsilon)$ is the set:

$$\{\gamma\,[r_2, c](f_c)\,[r_2, b](f_b),\ \gamma\,[r_2, b](f_b)\,[r_2, c](f_c)\}.$$

[6] using the usual concatenation $\circ$ of formal languages

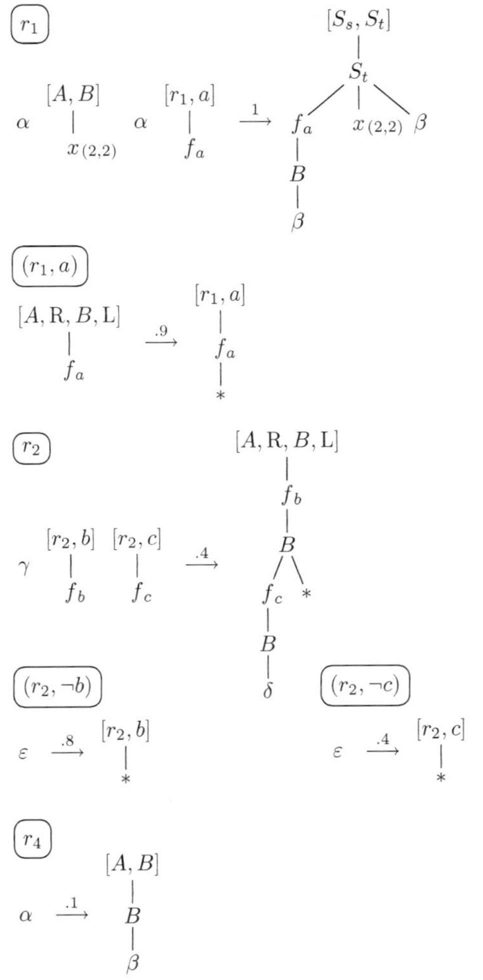

Figure 3: Some rules of the running example decoder.

Now let $\rho = \gamma\,[r_2, b](f_b)\,[r_2, c](f_c)$. Let us calculate $\psi_\rho(\varepsilon)$ on ζ_t.

$$\begin{aligned}\psi_\rho(\varepsilon) &\overset{(c)}{=} f_b(B(\psi_\rho(1), \psi_\rho(2)))\\ &\overset{(c)}{=} f_b(B(f_c(B(\psi_\rho(1.1))), \psi_\rho(2)))\\ &\overset{(a)}{=} f_b(B(f_c(B(\delta)), \psi_\rho(2)))\\ &\overset{(e)}{=} f_b(B(f_c(B(\delta)), *))\end{aligned}$$

Hence we obtain the rule

$$\gamma\,[r_2, b](f_b)\,[r_2, c](f_c) \to$$
$$[A, \mathrm{R}, B, \mathrm{L}](f_b(B(f_c(B(\delta)), *)))$$

which is also shown in Fig. 3.

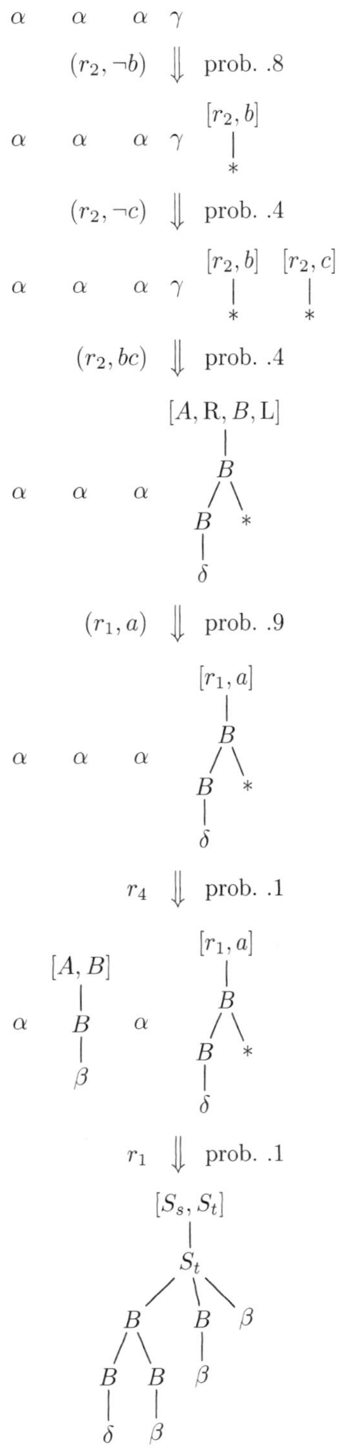

Figure 4: Derivation of the decoder corresponding to the derivation in Fig. 2.

References

A. Abeille, Y. Schabes, A.K. Joshi. Using lexicalized TAGs for machine translation. In *Proceedings of the 13th International Conference on Computational Linguistics*, volume 3, pp. 1–6, Helsinki, Finland, 1990.

C. Baier, M. Größer, F. Ciesinski. Model checking linear-time properties of probabilistic systems. In *Handbook of Weighted Automata*, Chapter 13, pp. 519–570, Springer, 2009.

S. DeNeefe. Tree adjoining machine translation. Ph.D. thesis proposal, Univ. of Southern California, 2009.

S. DeNeefe, K. Knight. Synchronous tree adjoining machine translation. In *Proc. of Conf. Empirical Methods in NLP*, pp. 727–736, 2009.

J. Engelfriet. Bottom-up and top-down tree transformations — a comparison. *Math. Systems Theory*, 9(3):198–231, 1975.

J. Engelfriet. Tree transducers and syntax-directed semantics. In *CAAP 1982: Lille, France*, 1982.

A. Fujiyoshi, T. Kasai. Spinal-formed context-free tree grammars. *Theory of Computing Systems*, 33:59–83, 2000.

Z. Fülöp, H. Vogler. Weighted tree automata and tree transducers. In *Handbook of Weighted Automata*, Chapter 9, pp. 313–403, Spinger, 2009.

F. Gécseg, M. Steinby. *Tree Automata*. Akadémiai Kiadó, Budapest, 1984.

F. Gécseg, M. Steinby. Tree languages. In *Handbook of Formal Languages*, volume 3, chapter 1, pages 1–68. Springer-Verlag, 1997.

J. Graehl, K. Knight, J. May. Training tree transducers. *Computational Linguistics*, 34(3):391–427, 2008

A.K. Joshi, L.S. Levy, M. Takahashi. Tree adjunct grammars. *Journal of Computer and System Sciences*, 10(1):136–163, 1975.

A.K. Joshi, Y. Schabes. Tree-adjoining grammars. In *Handbook of Formal Languages*. Chapter 2, pp. 69–123, Springer-Verlag, 1997.

K. Knight, J. Graehl. An overview of probabilistic tree transducers for natural language processing. In *Computational Linguistics and Intelligent Text Processing, CICLing 2005*, LNCS 3406, pp. 1–24, Springer, 2005.

K. Knight, J. May. Applications of Weighted Automata in Natural Language Processing. In *Handbook of Weighted Automata*, Chapter 14, pp. 571–596, Springer, 2009.

P.M. Lewis, R.E. Stearns. Syntax-directed transductions. *Journal of the ACM*, 15:465–488, 1968.

A. Maletti. Compositions of tree series transformations. *Theoret. Comput. Sci.*, 366:248–271, 2006.

A. Maletti. The Power of Tree Series Transducers. Ph.D. thesis, TU Dresden, Germany, 2006.

A. Maletti. Compositions of extended top-down tree transducers. *Information and Computation*, 206:1187–1196, 2008.

A. Maletti. Why synchronous tree substitution grammars? in *Proc. 11th Conf. North American Chapter of the Association of Computational Linguistics*. 2010.

D.F. Martin and S.A. Vere. On syntax-directed transductions and tree transducers. In *Ann. ACM Symposium on Theory of Computing*, pp. 129–135, 1970.

R. Nesson, S.M. Shieber, and A. Rush. Induction of probabilistic synchronous tree-insertion grammars. Technical Report TR-20-05, Computer Science Group, Harvard Univeristy, Cambridge, Massachusetts, 2005.

R. Nesson, S.M. Shieber, and A. Rush. Induction of probabilistic synchronous tree-inserting grammars for machine translation. In *Proceedings of the 7th Conference of the Association for Machine Translation in the Americas (AMTA 2006)*, 2006.

Y. Schabes, R.C. Waters. Tree insertion grammars: a cubic-time, parsable formalism that lexicalizes context-free grammar without changing the trees produced. *Computational Linguistics*, 21:479–513, 1994.

P.P. Schreiber. Tree-transducers and syntax-connected transductions. In *Automata Theory and Formal Languages*, Lecture Notes in Computer Science 33, pp. 202–208, Springer, 1975.

S.M. Shieber. Synchronous grammars and tree transducers. In *Proc. 7th Workshop on Tree Adjoining Grammars and Related Formalisms*, pp. 88–95, 2004.

S.M. Shieber. Unifying synchronous tree-adjoining grammars and tree transducers via bimorphisms. In *Proc. 11th Conf. European Chapter of ACL, EACL 06*, pp. 377–384, 2006.

S.M. Shieber, Y. Schabes. Synchronous tree-adjoining grammars. In *Proceedings of the 13th International Conference on Computational Linguistics*, volume 3, pp. 253–258, Helsinki, Finland, 1990.

K. Vijay-Shanker, D.J. Weir. The equivalence of four extensions of context-free grammars. *Mathematical Systems Theory*, 27:511–546, 1994.

K. Yamada and K. Knight. A syntax-based statistical translation model. In *Proc. of 39th Annual Meeting of the Assoc. Computational Linguistics*, pp. 523–530, 2001.

Parsing and Translation Algorithms Based on Weighted Extended Tree Transducers

Andreas Maletti[*]
Departament de Filologies Romàniques
Universitat Rovira i Virgili
Tarragona, Spain

Giorgio Satta
Department of Information Engineering
University of Padua
Padua, Italy

Abstract

This paper proposes a uniform framework for the development of parsing and translation algorithms for weighted extended (top-down) tree transducers and input strings. The asymptotic time complexity of these algorithms can be improved in practice by exploiting an algorithm for rule factorization in the above transducers.

1 Introduction

In the field of statistical machine translation, considerable interest has recently been shown for translation models based on weighted tree transducers. In this paper we consider the so-called weighted extended (top-down) tree transducers (WXTTs for short). WXTTs have been proposed by Graehl and Knight (2004) and Knight (2007) and are rooted in similar devices introduced earlier in the formal language literature (Arnold and Dauchet, 1982).

WXTTs have enough expressivity to represent hierarchical syntactic analyses for natural language sentences and can directly model most of the elementary operations that rule the process of translation between natural languages (Knight, 2007). Furthermore, the use of weights and internal states allows the encoding of statistical parameters that have recently been shown to be extremely useful in discriminating likely translations from less plausible ones.

For an WXTT M, the *parsing* problem is traditionally defined for a pair of trees t and u and requires as output some representation of the set of all computations of M that map t into u. Similarly, the *translation* problem for M is defined for an input tree t and requires as output some representation of the set of all computations of M mapping t into any other tree. When we deal with natural language processing applications, however, parsing and translation are most often represented on the basis of input strings rather than trees. Some tricks are then applied to map the problem back to the case of input trees. As an example in the context of machine translation, let w be some input string to be translated. One can intermediately construct a tree automaton M_w that recognizes the set of all possible trees that have w as yield with internal nodes from the input alphabet of M. This automaton M_w is further transformed into a tree transducer implementing a partial identity translation. This transducer is then composed with M (relational composition) to obtain a transducer that represents all translations of w. This is usually called the 'cascaded' approach.

In contrast with the cascaded approach above, which may be rather inefficient, we investigate a more direct technique for both parsing and translation of strings based on WXTTs. We do this by extending to WXTTs the well-known BAR-HILLEL construction defined for context-free grammars (Bar-Hillel et al., 1964) and for weighted context-free grammars (Nederhof and Satta, 2003). We then derive computational complexity results for parsing and translation of input strings on the basis of WXTTs. Finally, we develop a novel factorization algorithm for WXTTs that, in practical applications, can reduce the asymptotic complexity for such problems.

2 Preliminary definitions

Let $\cdot$ be an associative binary operation on a set S. If S contains an element 1 such that $1 \cdot s = s = s \cdot 1$ for every $s \in S$, then $(S, \cdot, 1)$ is a monoid. Such a monoid $(S, \cdot, 1)$ is commutative if the identity $s_1 \cdot s_2 = s_2 \cdot s_1$ holds for all $s_1, s_2 \in S$. A *commutative semiring* $(S, +, \cdot, 0, 1)$ is an algebraic structure such that:

- $(S, +, 0)$ and $(S, \cdot, 1)$ are commutative

[*]Financially supported by the *Ministerio de Educación y Ciencia* (MEC) grant JDCI-2007-760.

Proceedings of the 2010 Workshop on Applications of Tree Automata in Natural Language Processing, ACL 2010, pages 19–27, Uppsala, Sweden, 16 July 2010. ©2010 Association for Computational Linguistics

monoids,
- $\cdot$ distributes over $+$ (from both sides), and
- $s \cdot 0 = 0 = 0 \cdot s$ for every $s \in S$.

From now on, let $(S, +, \cdot, 0, 1)$ be a commutative semiring. An *alphabet* is a finite set of symbols. A *weighted string automaton* [WSA] (Schützenberger, 1961; Eilenberg, 1974) is a system $N = (P, \Gamma, J, \nu, F)$ where
- P and Γ are alphabets of states and input symbols, respectively,
- $J, F \colon P \to S$ assign initial and final weights, respectively, and
- $\nu \colon P \times \Gamma \times P \to S$ assigns a weight to each transition.

The transition weight mapping ν can be understood as square matrices $\nu(\cdot, \gamma, \cdot) \in S^{P \times P}$ for every $\gamma \in \Gamma$. The WSA N is *deterministic* if
- $J(p) \neq 0$ for at most one $p \in P$ and
- for every $p \in P$ and $\gamma \in \Gamma$ there exists at most one $p' \in P$ such that $\nu(p, \gamma, p') \neq 0$.

We now proceed with the semantics of N. We will define the *initial algebra semantics* here; alternative, equivalent definitions of the semantics exist (Sakarovitch, 2009). Let $w \in \Gamma^*$ be an input string, $\gamma \in \Gamma$, and $p, p' \in P$ be two states. We extend ν to a mapping $h_\nu \colon P \times \Gamma^* \times P \to S$ recursively as follows:

$$h_\nu(p, \varepsilon, p') = \begin{cases} 1 & \text{if } p = p' \\ 0 & \text{otherwise} \end{cases}$$

$$h_\nu(p, \gamma w, p') = \sum_{p'' \in P} \nu(p, \gamma, p'') \cdot h_\nu(p'', w, p') \ .$$

Consequently,

$$h_\nu(p, uw, p') = \sum_{p'' \in P} h_\nu(p, u, p'') \cdot h_\nu(p'', w, p')$$

for all $p, p' \in P$ and $u, w \in \Gamma^*$. Then the matrix $h_\nu(\cdot, \gamma_1 \cdots \gamma_k, \cdot)$ equals $\nu(\cdot, \gamma_1, \cdot) \cdot \ldots \cdot \nu(\cdot, \gamma_k, \cdot)$. Thus, if the semiring operations can be performed in constant time and access to $\nu(p, \gamma, q)$ is in constant time for every $p, q \in P$, then for every $w \in \Gamma^*$ we can compute the matrix $h_\nu(\cdot, w, \cdot)$ in time $\mathcal{O}(|w| \cdot |P|^3)$ because it can be computed by $|w| - 1$ matrix multiplications.

The WSA N computes the map $N \colon \Gamma^* \to S$, which is defined for every $w \in \Gamma^*$ by[1]

$$N(w) = \sum_{p, p' \in P} J(p) \cdot h_\nu(p, w, p') \cdot F(p') \ .$$

[1] We overload the symbol N to denote both the WSA and its recognized mapping. However, the intended meaning will always be clear from the context.

Since we will also consider individual runs, let us recall the run semantics as well. Let $w = \gamma_1 \cdots \gamma_k \in \Gamma^*$ be an input string of length k. Then any mapping $r \colon [0, k] \to P$ is a *run* of N on w, where $[0, k]$ denotes the set of integers between (inclusive) 0 and k. A run can be understood as a vector of states and thus we sometimes write r_i instead of $r(i)$. The weight of such a run r, denoted by $\mathrm{wt}_N(r)$, is defined by $\mathrm{wt}_N(r) = \prod_{i=1}^{k} \nu(r_{i-1}, \gamma_i, r_i)$. Then

$$h_\nu(p, w, p') = \sum_{\substack{r \colon [0,k] \to P \\ r_0 = p, r_k = p'}} \mathrm{wt}_N(r)$$

for every $p, p' \in P$ and $w \in \Gamma^*$.

3 Weighted extended tree transducers

Next, we move to tree languages, for which we need to introduce some additional notation. Let Σ be a *ranked alphabet*, that is, an alphabet whose symbols have a unique associated arity. We write Σ_k to denote the set of all k-ary symbols in Σ. We use the special nullary symbol $e \in \Sigma_0$ to syntactically represent the empty string ε. The set of Σ-*trees* indexed by a set V, denoted by $T_\Sigma(V)$, is the smallest set satisfying both of the following conditions:
- for every $v \in V$, the single node labeled v, written v, is a tree of $T_\Sigma(V)$,
- for every $\sigma \in \Sigma_k$ and $t_1, \ldots, t_k \in T_\Sigma(V)$, the tree with a root node labeled σ and trees $t_1, \ldots, t_k$ as its k children, written $\sigma(t_1, \ldots, t_k)$, belongs to $T_\Sigma(V)$.

Throughout this paper we sometimes write $\sigma()$ as just σ. In the following, let $t \in T_\Sigma(V)$. The set of *positions* $\mathrm{Pos}(t) \subseteq \mathbb{N}^*$ of a tree $t \in T_\Sigma(V)$ is recursively defined as follows:

$$\mathrm{Pos}(v) = \{\varepsilon\}$$

$$\mathrm{Pos}(t) = \{\varepsilon\} \cup \{iw \mid 1 \leq i \leq k, w \in \mathrm{Pos}(t_i)\}$$

for every $v \in V$, $\sigma \in \Sigma_k$, and $t_1, \ldots, t_k \in T_\Sigma(V)$ where $t = \sigma(t_1, \ldots, t_k)$. The label of t at position $w \in \mathrm{Pos}(t)$ is denoted by $t(w)$. The size of the tree $t \in T_\Sigma$ is defined as $|t| = |\mathrm{Pos}(t)|$. For every $w \in \mathrm{Pos}(t)$ the subtree of t that is rooted at w is denoted by $\mathrm{sub}_t(w)$; i.e.,

$$\mathrm{sub}_t(\varepsilon) = t$$

$$\mathrm{sub}_{\sigma(t_1, \ldots, t_k)}(iw) = \mathrm{sub}_{t_i}(w)$$

for every $\sigma \in \Sigma_k, t_1, \ldots, t_k \in T_\Sigma(V), 1 \leq i \leq k$, and $w \in \text{Pos}(t_i)$. Finally, the set of variables $\text{var}(t)$ is given by

$$\text{var}(t) = \{v \in V \mid \exists w \in \text{Pos}(t) \colon t(w) = v\} \ .$$

If for every $v \in \text{var}(t)$ there exists exactly one $w \in \text{Pos}(t)$ such that $t(w) = v$, then t is *linear*.

We use the fixed sets $X = \{x_i \mid i \geq 1\}$ and $Y = \{y_{i,j} \mid 1 \leq i < j\}$ of formal variables and the subsets $X_k = \{x_i \mid 1 \leq i \leq k\}$ and $Y_k = \{y_{i,j} \mid 1 \leq i < j \leq k\}$ for every $k \geq 0$. Note that $X_0 = \emptyset$. For every $H \subseteq \Sigma_0 \cup X \cup Y$, the H-yield of t is recursively defined by $\text{yd}_H(t) = t$ if $t \in H \setminus \{e\}$, $\text{yd}_H(t) = \text{yd}_H(t_1) \cdots \text{yd}_H(t_k)$ if $t = \sigma(t_1, \ldots, t_k)$ with $\sigma \in \Sigma_k$ and $k \geq 1$, and $\text{yd}_H(t) = \varepsilon$ otherwise. If $H = \Sigma_0 \cup X \cup Y$, then we also omit the index and just write $\text{yd}(t)$.

Let $l \in T_\Sigma(V)$ and $\theta \colon V \to T_\Sigma(V)$. Then $l\theta$ denotes the result obtained from l by replacing every occurrence of $v \in V$ by $\theta(v)$. The k-fold application is denoted by $l\theta^k$. If $l\theta^k = l\theta^{k+1}$ for some $k \geq 0$, then we denote $l\theta^k$ by $l\theta^*$. In addition, if $V = X_k$, then we write $l[\theta(x_1), \ldots, \theta(x_k)]$ instead of $l\theta$. We write $C_\Sigma(X_k)$ for the subset of those trees of $T_\Sigma(X_k)$ such that every variable of $x \in X_k$ occurs exactly once in it. Given $t \in T_\Sigma(X)$, we write $\text{dec}(t)$ for the set

$$\left\{(l, t_1, \ldots, t_k) \,\middle|\, \begin{array}{l} l \in C_\Sigma(X_k), l[t_1, \ldots, t_k] = t, \\ t_1, \ldots, t_k \in T_\Sigma(X) \end{array}\right\}$$

A *(linear and nondeleting) weighted extended (top-down) tree transducer* [WXTT] (Arnold and Dauchet, 1975; Arnold and Dauchet, 1976; Lilin, 1981; Arnold and Dauchet, 1982; Maletti et al., 2009) is a system $M = (Q, \Sigma, \Delta, I, R)$ where

- Q is an alphabet of states,
- Σ and Δ are ranked alphabets of input and output symbols, respectively,
- $I \colon Q \to S$ assigns initial weights, and
- R is a finite set of rules of the form $(q, l) \xrightarrow{s} (q_1 \cdots q_k, r)$ with $q, q_1, \ldots, q_k \in Q$, $l \in C_\Sigma(X_k)$ and $r \in C_\Delta(X_k)$, and $s \in S$ such that $\{l, r\} \nsubseteq X$.

Let us discuss the final restriction imposed on the rules of a WXTT. Essentially, it disallows rules of the form $(q, x_1) \xrightarrow{s} (q', x_1)$ with $q, q' \in Q$ and $s \in S$. Such *pure epsilon rules* only change the state and charge a cost. However, they can yield infinite derivations (and with it infinite products and sums) and are not needed in our applications. The WXTT M is *standard* if $\text{yd}_X(r) = x_1 \cdots x_k$ for every $(q, l) \xrightarrow{s} (q_1 \cdots q_k, r) \in R$. This restriction enforces that the order of the variables is fixed on the right-hand side r, but since the order is arbitrary in the left-hand side l (and the names of the variables are inconsequential), it can be achieved easily without loss of generality. If there are several rules that differ only in the naming of the variables, then their weights should be added to obtain a single standard rule. To keep the presentation simple, we also construct nonstandard WXTTs in the sequel. However, we implicitly assume that those are converted into standard WXTTs.

The semantics of a standard WXTT is inspired by the initial-algebra semantics for classical weighted top-down and bottom-up tree transducers (Fülöp and Vogler, 2009) [also called top-down and bottom-up tree series transducers by Engelfriet et al. (2002)]. Note that our semantics is equivalent to the classical term rewriting semantics, which is presented by Graehl and Knight (2004) and Graehl et al. (2008), for example. In fact, we will present an equivalent semantics based on runs later. Let $M = (Q, \Sigma, \Delta, I, R)$ be a WXTT. We present a definition that is more general than immediately necessary, but the generalization will be useful later on. For every $n \in \mathbb{N}$, $p_1, \ldots, p_n \in Q$, and $L \subseteq R$, we define the mapping $h_L^{p_1 \cdots p_n} \colon T_\Sigma(X_n) \times T_\Delta(X_n) \to S^Q$ by $h_L^{p_1 \cdots p_n}(x_i, x_i)_{p_i} = 1$ for every $1 \leq i \leq n$ and

$$h_L^{p_1 \cdots p_n}(t, u)_q = \sum_{\substack{(l, t_1, \ldots, t_k) \in \text{dec}(t) \\ (r, u_1, \ldots, u_k) \in \text{dec}(u) \\ (q, l) \xrightarrow{s} (q_1 \cdots q_k, r) \in L}} s \cdot \prod_{i=1}^{k} h_L^{p_1 \cdots p_n}(t_i, u_i)_{q_i} \quad (1)$$

for all remaining $t \in T_\Sigma(X_n)$, $u \in T_\Delta(X_n)$, and $q \in Q$. Note that for each nonzero summand in (1) one of the decompositions $\text{dec}(t)$ and $\text{dec}(u)$ must be proper (i.e., either $l \notin X$ or $r \notin X$). This immediately yields that the sum is finite and the recursion well-defined. The transformation computed by M, also denoted by M, is the mapping $M \colon T_\Sigma \times T_\Delta \to S$, which is defined by $M(t, u) = \sum_{q \in Q} I(q) \cdot h_R(t, u)_q$ for every $t \in T_\Sigma$ and $u \in T_\Delta$.

Let us also introduce a run semantics for the WXTT $(Q, \Sigma, \Delta, I, R)$. The rank of a rule $\rho = (q, l) \xrightarrow{s} (q_1 \cdots q_k, r) \in R$, denoted by $\text{rk}(\rho)$, is $\text{rk}(\rho) = k$. This turns R into a ranked alphabet. The input state of ρ is $\text{in}(\rho) = q$, the ith output state is $\text{out}_i(\rho) = q_i$ for every $1 \leq i \leq k$, and the weight of ρ is $\mathrm{wt}(\rho) = s$. A tree $r \in T_R(X)$ is called *run* if $\mathrm{in}(r(wi)) = \mathrm{out}_i(r(w))$ for every $wi \in \mathrm{Pos}(r)$ and $1 \leq i \leq \mathrm{rk}(r(w))$ such that $r(wi) \in R$. The weight of a run $r \in T_R(X)$ is

$$\mathrm{wt}(r) = \prod_{w \in \mathrm{Pos}(r), r(w) \in R} \mathrm{wt}(r(w)) \ .$$

The evaluation mappings $\pi_1 \colon T_R(X) \to T_\Sigma(X)$ and $\pi_2 \colon T_R(X) \to T_\Delta(X)$ are defined for every $x \in X$, $\rho = (q, l) \xrightarrow{s} (q_1 \cdots q_k, r) \in R$, and $r_1, \dots, r_k \in T_R(X)$ by $\pi_1(x) = x$, $\pi_2(x) = x$, and

$$\pi_1(\rho(r_1, \dots, r_k)) = l[\pi_1(r_1), \dots, \pi_1(r_k)]$$
$$\pi_2(\rho(r_1, \dots, r_k)) = r[\pi_2(r_1), \dots, \pi_2(r_k)] \ .$$

We obtain the weighted tree transformation for every $t \in T_\Sigma$ and $u \in T_\Delta$ as follows[2]

$$M(t, u) = \sum_{\substack{\text{run } r \in T_R \\ t = \pi_1(r), u = \pi_2(r)}} I(\mathrm{in}(r(\varepsilon))) \cdot \mathrm{wt}(r) \ .$$

This approach is also called the *bimorphism approach* (Arnold and Dauchet, 1982) to tree transformations.

4 Input and output restrictions of WXTT

In this section we will discuss the BAR-HILLEL construction for the input and the output part of a WXTT M. This construction essentially restricts the input or output of the WXTT M to the string language recognized by a WSA N. Contrary to (direct or inverse) application, this construction is supposed to yield another WXTT. More precisely, the constructed WXTT should assign to each translation (t, u) the weight assigned to it by M multiplied by the weight assigned by N to the yield of t (or u if the output is restricted). Since our WXTTs are symmetric, we will actually only need one construction. Let us quickly establish the mentioned symmetry statement. Essentially we just have to exchange left- and right-hand sides and redistribute the states in those left- and right-hand sides accordingly.

From now on, let $M = (Q, \Sigma, \Delta, I, R)$ be a WXTT.

Theorem 1. *There exists a WXTT M' such that $M'(u, t) = M(t, u)$ for every $t \in T_\Sigma$ and $u \in T_\Delta$.*

[2]We immediately also use M for the run semantics because the two semantics trivially coincide.

Proof. Let $M' = (Q, \Delta, \Sigma, I, R')$ be the WXTT such that

$$R' = \{(q, r) \xrightarrow{s} (w, l) \mid (q, l) \xrightarrow{s} (w, r) \in R\} \ .$$

It should be clear that $M'(u, t) = M(t, u)$ for every $t \in T_\Sigma$ and $u \in T_\Delta$. □

With the symmetry established, we now only need to present the BAR-HILLEL construction for either the input or output side. Without loss of generality, let us assume that M is standard. We then choose the output side here because the order of variables is fixed in it. Note that we sometimes use the angled parentheses '⟨' and '⟩' instead of parentheses for clarity.

Definition 2. *Let $N = (P, \Gamma, J, \nu, F)$ be a WSA with $\Gamma = \Delta_0 \setminus \{e\}$. We construct the output product $\mathrm{Prod}(M, N) = (P \times Q \times P, \Sigma, \Delta, I', R')$ such that*

- *$I'(\langle p, q, p' \rangle) = J(p) \cdot I(q) \cdot F(p')$ for every $p, p' \in P$ and $q \in Q$,*
- *for every rule $(q, l) \xrightarrow{s} (q_1 \cdots q_k, r) \in R$ and every $p_0, \dots, p_k, p'_0, \dots, p'_k \in P$, let*

$$(q', l) \xrightarrow{s \cdot s_0 \cdot \ldots \cdot s_k} (q'_1 \cdots q'_k, r) \in R'$$

where

- $q' = \langle p_0, q, p'_k \rangle$,
- $q'_i = \langle p'_{i-1}, q_i, p_i \rangle$ *for every* $1 \leq i \leq k$,
- $\mathrm{yd}(r) = w_0 x_1 w_1 \cdots w_{k-1} x_k w_k$ *with* $w_0, \dots, w_k \in \Gamma^*$, *and*
- $s_i = h_\nu(p_i, w_i, p'_i)$ *for every* $0 \leq i \leq k$.

Let $\rho = (q, l) \xrightarrow{s} (q_1 \cdots q_k, r) \in R$. The *size* of ρ is $|\rho| = |l| + |r|$. The size and rank of the WXTT M are $|M| = \sum_{\rho \in R} |\rho|$ and $\mathrm{rk}(M) = \max_{\rho \in R} \mathrm{rk}(\rho)$, respectively. Finally, the maximal output yield length of M, denoted by $\mathrm{len}(M)$, is the maximal length of $\mathrm{yd}(r)$ for all rules $(q, l) \xrightarrow{s} (q_1 \cdots q_k, r) \in R$. The size and rank of $\mathrm{Prod}(M, N)$ are in $\mathcal{O}(|M| \cdot |P|^{2\,\mathrm{rk}(M)+2})$ and $\mathrm{rk}(M)$, respectively. We can compute $\mathrm{Prod}(M, N)$ in time $\mathcal{O}(|R| \cdot \mathrm{len}(M) \cdot |P|^{2\,\mathrm{rk}(M)+5})$. If N is deterministic, then the size of $\mathrm{Prod}(M, N)$ is in $\mathcal{O}(|M| \cdot |P|^{\mathrm{rk}(M)+1})$ and the required time is in $\mathcal{O}(|R| \cdot \mathrm{len}(M) \cdot |P|^{\mathrm{rk}(M)+1})$. Next, let us prove that our BAR-HILLEL construction is actually correct.

Theorem 3. *Let M and N be as in Definition 2, and let $M' = \mathrm{Prod}(M, N)$. Then $M'(t, u) = M(t, u) \cdot N(\mathrm{yd}(u))$ for every $t \in T_\Sigma$ and $u \in T_\Delta$.*

Proof. Let $M' = (Q', \Sigma, \Delta, I', R')$. First, a simple proof shows that

$$h_{R'}(t,u)_{\langle p,q,p'\rangle} = h_R(t,u)_q \cdot h_\nu(p, \mathrm{yd}(u), p')$$

for every $t \in T_\Sigma$, $u \in T_\Delta$, $q \in Q$, and $p, p' \in P$. Now we can prove the main statement as follows:

$$\begin{aligned} & M'(t,u) \\ = & \sum_{q' \in Q'} I'(q') \cdot h_{R'}(t,u)_{q'} \\ = & \sum_{\substack{p,p' \in P \\ q \in Q}} I'(\langle p,q,p'\rangle) \cdot h_R(t,u)_q \cdot h_\nu(p, \mathrm{yd}(u), p') \\ = & M(t,u) \cdot N(\mathrm{yd}(u)) \end{aligned}$$

for every $t \in T_\Sigma$ and $u \in T_\Delta$. □

Note that the typical property of many BAR-HILLEL constructions, namely that a run of M and a run of N uniquely determine a run of $\mathrm{Prod}(M, N)$ and vice versa, does not hold for our construction. In fact, a run of M and a run of N uniquely determine a run of $\mathrm{Prod}(M, N)$, but the converse does not hold. We could modify the construction to enable this property at the expense of an exponential increase in the number of states of $\mathrm{Prod}(M, N)$. However, since those relations are important for our applications, we explore the relation between runs in some detail here.

To simplify the discussion, we assume, without loss of generality, that M is standard and $s = s'$ for every two rules $(q,l) \xrightarrow{s} (w,r) \in R$ and $(q,l) \xrightarrow{s'} (w,r) \in R$. Moreover, we assume the symbols of Definition 2. For every $r' \in T_{R'}(X)$, we let $\mathrm{base}(r')$ denote the run obtained from r' by replacing each symbol

$$(q', l) \xrightarrow{s \cdot s_0 \cdot \ldots \cdot s_k} (q'_1 \cdots q'_k, r)$$

by just $(q, l) \xrightarrow{s} (q_1 \cdots q_k, r) \in R$. Thus, we replace a rule (which is a symbol) of R' by the underlying rule of R. We start with a general lemma, which we believe to be self-evident.

Lemma 4. *Let $r' \in T_{R'}$ and $n = |\mathrm{yd}(\pi_2(r'))|$. Then $\mathrm{wt}_{M'}(r') = \mathrm{wt}_M(\mathrm{base}(r')) \cdot \sum_{r \in R''} \mathrm{wt}_N(r)$ where R'' is a nonempty subset of $\{r \colon [0,n] \to P \mid \mathrm{in}(r'(\varepsilon)) = \langle r_0, q, r_n\rangle\}$.*

Let us assume that N is trim (i.e., all states are reachable and co-reachable) and unambiguous. In this case, for every $\gamma_1 \cdots \gamma_k \in \Gamma^*$ and $p, p' \in P$ there is at most one successful run $r \colon [0,k] \to P$ such that

- $\nu(r_{i-1}, \gamma_i, r_i) \neq 0$ for every $1 \leq i \leq k$, and
- $r_0 = p$ and $r_k = p'$.

This immediately yields the following corollary.

Corollary 5 (of Lemma 4). *Let N be trim and unambiguous. For every $r' \in T_{R'}$ we have*

$$\mathrm{wt}_{M'}(r') = \mathrm{wt}_M(\mathrm{base}(r')) \cdot \mathrm{wt}_N(r)$$

for some $r \colon [0,n] \to P$ with $n = |\mathrm{yd}(\pi_2(r'))|$.

We now turn to applications of the product construction. We first consider the translation problem for an input string w and a WXTT M. We can represent w as a trim and unambiguous WSA N_w that recognizes the language $\{w\}$ with weight of 1 on each transition (which amounts to ignoring the weight contribution of N_w). Then the input product transducer $M_w = \mathrm{Prod}(N_w, M)$ provides a compact representation of the set of all computations of M that translate the string w. From Corollary 5 we have that the weights of these computations are also preserved. Thus, $M_w(T_\Sigma \times T_\Delta) = \sum_{(t,u) \in T_\Sigma \times T_\Delta} M_w(t,u)$ is the weight of the set of string translations of w.

As usual in natural language processing applications, we can exploit appropriate semirings and compute several useful statistical parameters through $M_w(T_\Sigma \times T_\Delta)$, as for instance the highest weight of a computation, the inside probability and the rule expectations; see (Li and Eisner, 2009) for further discussion.

One could also construct in linear time the range tree automaton for M_w, which can be interpreted as a parsing forest with all the weighted trees assigned to translations of w under M. If we further assume that M is unambiguous, then M_w will also have this property, and we can apply standard techniques to extract from M_w the highest score computation. In machine translation applications, the unambiguity assumption is usually met, and avoids the so-called 'spurious' ambiguity, that is, having several computations for an individual pair of trees.

The parsing problem for input strings w and u can be treated in a similar way, by restricting M both to the left and to the right.

5 Rule factorization

As already discussed, the time complexity of the product construction is an exponential function of the rank of the transducer. Unfortunately, it is not possible in the general case to cast a

WXTT into a normal form such that the rank is bounded by some constant. This is also expected from the fact that the translation problem for subclasses of WXTTs such as synchronous context-free grammars is NP-hard (Satta and Peserico, 2005). Nonetheless, there are cases in which a rank reduction is possible, which might result in an improvement of the asymptotical run-time of our construction.

Following the above line, we present here a linear time algorithm for reducing the rank of a WXTT under certain conditions. Similar algorithms for tree-based transformation devices have been discussed in the literature. Nesson et al. (2008) consider synchronous tree adjoining grammars; their algorithm is conceptually very similar to ours, but computationally more demanding due to the treatment of adjunction. Following that work, we also demand here that the new WXTT 'preserves' the recursive structure of the input WXTT, as formalized below. Galley et al. (2004) algorithm also behaves in linear time, but deals with the different problem of tree to string translation. Rank reduction algorithms for string-based translation devices have also been discussed by Zhang et al. (2006) and Gildea et al. (2006).

Recall that $M = (Q, \Sigma, \Delta, I, R)$ is a standard WXTT. Let $M' = (Q', \Sigma, \Delta, I', R')$ be a WXTT with $Q \subseteq Q'$.[3] Then M' is a *structure-preserving factorization* of M if

- $I'(q) = I(q)$ for every $q \in Q$ and $I'(q) = 0$ otherwise, and
- $h_{R'}^{p_1 \cdots p_n}(t, u)_q = h_R^{p_1 \cdots p_n}(t, u)_q$ for every $q, p_1, \ldots, p_n \in Q$, $t \in T_\Sigma(X_n)$, and $u \in T_\Delta(X_n)$.

In particular, we have $h_{R'}(t, u)_q = h_R(t, u)_q$ for $n = 0$. Consequently, M' and M are equivalent because

$$M'(t, u) = \sum_{q \in Q'} I'(q) \cdot h_{R'}(t, u)_q = \sum_{q \in Q} I(q) \cdot h_R(t, u)_q = M(t, u) \ .$$

Note that the relation 'is structure-preserving factorization of' is reflexive and transitive, and thus, a pre-order. Moreover, in a ring (actually, additively cancellative semirings are sufficient) it is also antisymmetric, and consequently, a partial order.

[3] Actually, an injective mapping $Q \to Q'$ would be sufficient, but since the naming of the states is arbitrary, we immediately identify according to the injective mapping.

Informally, a structure-preserving factorization of M consists in a set of new rules that can be composed to provide the original rules and preserve their weights. We develop an algorithm for finding a structure-preserving factorization by decomposing each rule as much as possible. The algorithm can then be iterated for all the rules in the WXTT. The idea underlying our algorithm is very simple. Let $\rho = (q, l) \xrightarrow{s} (q_1 \cdots q_k, r) \in R$ be an original rule. We look for subtrees l' and r' of l and r, respectively, such that $\mathrm{var}(l') = \mathrm{var}(r')$. The condition that $\mathrm{var}(l') = \mathrm{var}(r')$ is derived from the fact that $h_R^{q_1 \cdots q_k}(l', r')_q = 0$ if $\mathrm{var}(l') \neq \mathrm{var}(r')$. We then split ρ into two new rules by 'excising' subtrees l' and r' from l and r, respectively. In the remaining trees the 'excised' trees are replaced with some fresh variable. The tricky part is the efficient computation of the pairs (w_l, w_r), since in the worst case the number of such pairs is in $\Theta(|l| \cdot |r|)$, and naïve testing of the condition $\mathrm{var}(l') = \mathrm{var}(r')$ takes time $\mathcal{O}(\mathrm{rk}(\rho))$.

Let us start with the formal development. Recall the doubly-indexed set $Y = \{y_{i,j} \mid 1 \leq i < j\}$. Intuitively speaking, the variable $y_{i,j}$ will represent the set $\{x_i, \ldots, x_j\}$. With this intuition in mind, we define the mapping $\mathrm{vars}\colon T_\Sigma(X \cup Y) \to \mathbb{N}_\infty^3$ as follows:

$$\mathrm{vars}(x_i) = (i, i, 1)$$
$$\mathrm{vars}(y_{i,j}) = (i, j, j - i + 1)$$

and $\mathrm{vars}(\sigma(t_1, \ldots, t_k))$ is

$$(\min_{\ell=1}^{k} \mathrm{vars}(t_\ell)_1, \max_{\ell=1}^{k} \mathrm{vars}(t_\ell)_2, \sum_{\ell=1}^{k} \mathrm{vars}(t_\ell)_3)$$

for every $i, j \in \mathbb{N}$ with $i < j$, $\sigma \in \Sigma_k$, and $t_1, \ldots, t_k \in T_\Sigma(X \cup Y)$. Clearly, $\mathrm{vars}(t)$ can be computed in time $\mathcal{O}(|t|)$, which also includes the computation of $\mathrm{vars}(u)$ for every subtree u of t. In addition, $\mathrm{vars}(t)_3 = |\mathrm{var}(t)|$ for all linear $t \in T_\Sigma(X)$. Finally, if $t \in T_\Sigma(X)$, then $\mathrm{vars}(t)_1$ and $\mathrm{vars}(t)_2$ are the minimal and maximal index $i \in \mathbb{N}$ such that $x_i \in \mathrm{var}(t)$, respectively (they are ∞ and 0, respectively, if $\mathrm{var}(t) = \emptyset$). For better readability, we use $\mathrm{minvar}(t)$ and $\mathrm{maxvar}(t)$ for $\mathrm{vars}(t)_1$ and $\mathrm{vars}(t)_2$, respectively.

Let $\rho = (q, l) \xrightarrow{s} (q_1 \cdots q_k, r) \in R$ be an original rule. In the following, we will use $\mathrm{minvar}(t)$, $\mathrm{maxvar}(t)$, and $|\mathrm{var}(t)|$ freely for all subtrees t of l and r and assume that they are precomputed, which can be done in time $\mathcal{O}(|\rho|)$. Moreover, we will freely use the test 'var(t) = var(u)' for subtrees t and u of l and r, respectively. This test can be performed in constant time [disregarding the time needed to precompute vars(t) and vars(u)] by the equivalent test

- $\mathrm{minvar}(t) = \mathrm{minvar}(u)$,
- $\mathrm{maxvar}(t) = \mathrm{maxvar}(u)$,
- $|\mathrm{var}(t)| = \mathrm{maxvar}(t) - \mathrm{minvar}(t) + 1$, and
- $|\mathrm{var}(u)| = \mathrm{maxvar}(u) - \mathrm{minvar}(u) + 1$.

Our factorization algorithm is presented in Algorithm 1. Its first two parameters hold the left- and right-hand side (l, r), which are to be decomposed. The third and fourth parameter should initially be x_1. To simplify the algorithm, we assume that it is only called with left- and right-hand sides that (i) contain the same variables and (ii) contain at least two variables. These conditions are ensured by the algorithm for the recursive calls. The algorithm returns a decomposition of (l, r) in the form of a set $\mathcal{D} \subseteq T_\Sigma(X \cup Y) \times T_\Delta(X \cup Y)$ such that $\mathrm{var}(l') = \mathrm{var}(r')$ for every $(l', r') \in \mathcal{D}$. Moreover, all such l' and r' are linear. Finally, the pairs in $\mathcal{D}$ can be composed (by means of point-wise substitution at the variables of Y) to form the original pair (l, r).

Before we move on to formal properties of Algorithm 1, let us illustrate its execution on an example.

Example 6. *We work with the left-hand side* $l = \sigma(x_1, \sigma(x_3, x_2))$ *and the right-hand side* $r = \gamma(\sigma(x_1, \gamma(\sigma(x_2, x_3))))$. *Then* $|\mathrm{var}(l)| \geq 2$ *and* $\mathrm{var}(l) = \mathrm{var}(r)$. *Let us trace the call* $\textsc{Decompose}(l, r, x_1, x_1)$. *The condition in line 1 is clearly false, so we proceed with line 3. The condition is true for* $i = 1$, *so we continue with* $\textsc{Decompose}(l, \sigma(x_1, \gamma(\sigma(x_2, x_3))), x_1, \gamma(x_1))$.

This time neither the condition in line 1 nor the condition in line 3 are true. In line 6, j *is set to 1 and we initialize* $r'_1 = x_1$ *and* $r'_2 = \gamma(\sigma(x_2, x_3))$. *Moreover, the array* h *is initialized to* $h(1) = 1$, $h(2) = 2$, *and* $h(3) = 2$. *Now let us discuss the main loop starting in line 12 in more detail. First, we consider* $i = 1$. *Since* $l_1 = x_1$, *the condition in line 13 is fulfilled and we set* $l'_1 = x_1$ *and proceed with the next iteration* ($i = 2$). *This time the condition of line 13 is false because* $l_2 = \sigma(x_3, x_2)$ *and* $\mathrm{var}(l_2) = \mathrm{var}(r_{h(2)}) = \mathrm{var}(r_2) = \{x_2, x_3\}$. *Consequently,* j *is set to 2 and* $l'_2 = r'_2 = y_{2,3}$. *Next,* $\textsc{Decompose}(\sigma(x_3, x_2), \gamma(\sigma(x_2, x_3)), x_1, x_1)$ *is processed. Let us suppose that it generates the set* $\mathcal{D}$. *Then we return*

$$\mathcal{D} \cup \{(\sigma(x_1, y_{2,3}), \gamma(\sigma(x_1, y_{2,3})))\} \enspace .$$

Finally, let us quickly discuss how the set $\mathcal{D}$ *is obtained. Since the condition in line 3 is true, we have to evaluate the recursive call* $\textsc{Decompose}(\sigma(x_3, x_2), \sigma(x_2, x_3), x_1, \gamma(x_1))$.

Now, $j = 2$, $h(2) = 1$, *and* $h(3) = 2$. *Moreover,* $r'_1 = x_2$ *and* $r'_2 = x_3$. *In the main loop starting in line 12, the condition of line 13 is always fulfilled, which yields that* $l'_1 = x_3$ *and* $l'_2 = x_2$. *Thus, we return* $\{(\sigma(x_3, x_2), \gamma(\sigma(x_2, x_3)))\}$, *which is exactly the input because decomposition completely failed. Thus, the overall decomposition of* l *and* r *is*

$$\{(\sigma(x_1, y_{2,3}), \gamma(\sigma(x_1, y_{2,3}))),\\ (\sigma(x_3, x_2), \gamma(\sigma(x_2, x_3)))\} \enspace ,$$

which, when the second pair is substituted (point-wise) for $y_{2,3}$ *in the first pair, yields exactly* (l, r).

Informally, the rules are obtained as follows from $\mathcal{D}$. If all variables occur in a pair $(l', r') \in \mathcal{D}$, then the left-hand side is assigned to the original input state. Furthermore, for every variable $y_{i,j}$ we introduce a new fresh state $q_{i,j}$ whereas the variable x_i is associated to q_i. In this way, we determine the states in the right-hand side.

Formally, let $\rho = (q, l) \xrightarrow{s} (q_1 \cdots q_k, r)$ be the original rule and $\mathcal{D}$ be the result of $\textsc{Decompose}(l, r, x_1, x_1)$ of Algorithm 1. In addition, for every $1 \leq i < j \leq k$, let $q_{\rho,i,j}$ be a new state such that $q_{\rho,1,k} = q$. Let

$$Q'_\rho = \{q, q_1, \ldots, q_k\} \cup \{q_{\rho,i,j} \mid 1 \leq i < j \leq k\} \enspace .$$

Then for every $(l', r') \in \mathcal{D}$ we obtain the rule

$$(q_{\rho,\mathrm{minvar}(r'),\mathrm{maxvar}(r')}, l') \xrightarrow{s'} (p_1 \cdots p_n, r')$$

where $\mathrm{yd}_{X \cup Y}(r') = z_1 \cdots z_n$,

$$s' = \begin{cases} s & \text{if } \mathrm{vars}(r')_3 = k \\ 1 & \text{otherwise} \end{cases}$$

$$q'_\ell = \begin{cases} q_j & \text{if } z_\ell = x_j \\ q_{\rho,i,j} & \text{if } z_\ell = y_{i,j} \end{cases}$$

for every $1 \leq \ell \leq n$. The rules obtained in this fashion are collected in R'_ρ.[4] The WXTT $\mathrm{dec}(M)$ is $\mathrm{dec}(M) = (Q', \Sigma, \Delta, I', R')$ where

[4]Those rules need to be normalized to obtain a standard WXTT.

Algorithm 1 DECOMPOSE(l, r, l', r') computing the decomposition of linear $l \in T_\Sigma(X_k)$ and $r \in T_\Delta(X_k)$ with $\text{var}(l) = \text{var}(r)$ and $|\text{var}(l)| \geq 2$.

if $l = \sigma(l_1, \ldots, l_m)$ and there exists $i \in \mathbb{N}$ is such that $\text{var}(l_i) = \text{var}(l)$ **then**
2: **return** DECOMPOSE$(l_i, r, l'[\sigma(l_1, \ldots, l_{i-1}, x_1, l_{i+1}, \ldots, l_m)], r'[x_1])$
if $r = \delta(r_1, \ldots, r_n)$ and there exists $i \in \mathbb{N}$ is such that $\text{var}(r_i) = \text{var}(r)$ **then**
4: **return** DECOMPOSE$(l, r_i, l'[x_1], r'[\delta(r_1, \ldots, r_{i-1}, x_1, r_{i+1}, \ldots, r_n)])$
let $l = \sigma(l_1, \ldots, l_m)$ and $r = \delta(r_1, \ldots, r_n)$
6: $j = \text{minvar}(r)$
for all $1 \leq i \leq n$ **do**
8: $r'_i = r_i$
while $j \leq \text{maxvar}(r_i)$ **do**
10: $h(j) = i; j = j + 1$
$\mathcal{D} = \emptyset$
12: **for all** $1 \leq i \leq m$ **do**
if $|\text{var}(l_i)| \leq 1$ or $\text{var}(l_i) \neq \text{var}(r_{h(\text{minvar}(l_i))})$ **then**
14: $l'_i = l_i$
else
16: $j = h(\text{minvar}(l_i))$
$l'_i = r'_j = y_{\text{minvar}(l_i), \text{maxvar}(l_i)}$
18: $\mathcal{D} = \mathcal{D} \cup$ DECOMPOSE(l_i, r_j, x_1, x_1)
return $\mathcal{D} \cup \{(l'[\sigma(l'_1, \ldots, l'_m)], r'[\delta(r'_1, \ldots, r'_n)])\}$

- $Q' = Q \cup \bigcup_{\rho \in R, \text{rk}(\rho) \geq 2} Q'_\rho$,
- $I'(q) = I(q)$ for every $q \in Q$ and $I'(q) = 0$ otherwise, and
- R' is

$$\{\rho \in R \mid \text{rk}(\rho) < 2\} \cup \bigcup_{\rho \in R, \text{rk}(\rho) \geq 2} R'_\rho \ .$$

To measure the success of the factorization, we introduce the following notion. The degree of M, denoted by $\deg(M)$, is the minimal rank of all structure-preserving factorizations M' of M; i.e.,

$$\deg(M) = \min_{\substack{M' \text{ a structure-preserving} \\ \text{factorization of } M}} \text{rk}(M') \ .$$

Then the goal of this section is the efficient computation of a structure-preserving factorization M' of M such that $\text{rk}(M') = \deg(M)$.

Theorem 7. *The WXTT* $\text{dec}(M)$ *is a structure-preserving factorization of* M *such that* $\text{rk}(\text{dec}(M)) = \deg(M)$. *Moreover,* $\text{dec}(M)$ *can be computed in time* $\mathcal{O}(|M|)$.

Proof. Let us only discuss the run-time complexity shortly. Clearly, DECOMPOSE(l, r, x_1, x_1) should be called once for each rule $(q, l) \xrightarrow{s} (q_1 \cdots q_k, r) \in R$. In lines 1–4 the structure of l and r is inspected and the properties $\text{var}(l_i) = \text{var}(l)$ and $\text{var}(r_i) = \text{var}(r)$ are tested in constant time. Mind that we precomputed $\text{vars}(l)$ and $\text{vars}(r)$, which can be done in linear time in the size of the rule. Then each subtree r_i is considered in lines 7–10 in constant time. Finally, we consider all direct input subtrees l_i in lines 12–18. The tests involving the variables are all performed in constant time due to the preprocessing step that computes $\text{vars}(l)$ and $\text{vars}(r)$. Moreover, at most one recursive call to DECOMPOSE is generated for each input subtree t_i. So if we implement the union in lines 18 and 19 by a constant-time operation (such as list concatenation, which can be done since it is trivially a disjoint union), then we obtain the linear time-complexity. □

6 Concluding remarks

In this paper we have shown how to restrict computations of WXTTs to given input and output WSA, and have discussed the relevance of this technique for parsing and translation applications over input strings, resulting in the computation of translation forests and other statistical parameters of interest. We have also shown how to factorize transducer rules, resulting in an asymptotic reduction in the complexity for these algorithms.

In machine translation applications transducers usually have very large sets of rules. One should then specialize the restriction construction in such a way that the number of useless rules for $\text{Prod}(N_w, M)$ is considerably reduced, resulting in a more efficient construction. This can be achieved by grounding the construction of the new rules by means of specialized strategies, as usually done for parsing based on context-free grammars; see for instance the parsing algorithms by Younger (1967) or by Earley (1970).

References

André Arnold and Max Dauchet. 1975. *Transductions inversibles de forêts*. Thèse 3ème cycle M. Dauchet, Université de Lille.

André Arnold and Max Dauchet. 1976. Bi-transductions de forêts. In *ICALP*, pages 74–86. Edinburgh University Press.

André Arnold and Max Dauchet. 1982. Morphismes et bimorphismes d'arbres. *Theoret. Comput. Sci.*, 20(1):33–93.

Yehoshua Bar-Hillel, Micha Perles, and Eliyahu Shamir. 1964. On formal properties of simple phrase structure grammars. In Yehoshua Bar-Hillel, editor, *Language and Information: Selected Essays on their Theory and Application*, chapter 9, pages 116–150. Addison Wesley.

Jay Earley. 1970. An efficient context-free parsing algorithm. *Commun. ACM*, 13(2):94–102.

Samuel Eilenberg. 1974. *Automata, Languages, and Machines*, volume 59 of *Pure and Applied Math.* Academic Press.

Joost Engelfriet, Zoltán Fülöp, and Heiko Vogler. 2002. Bottom-up and top-down tree series transformations. *J. Autom. Lang. Combin.*, 7(1):11–70.

Zoltán Fülöp and Heiko Vogler. 2009. Weighted tree automata and tree transducers. In Manfred Droste, Werner Kuich, and Heiko Vogler, editors, *Handbook of Weighted Automata*, EATCS Monographs on Theoret. Comput. Sci., chapter IX, pages 313–403. Springer.

Michel Galley, Mark Hopkins, Kevin Knight, and Daniel Marcu. 2004. What's in a translation rule? In *Proc. HLT-NAACL*, pages 273–280. Association for Computational Linguistics.

Daniel Gildea, Giorgio Satta, and Hao Zhang. 2006. Factoring synchronous grammars by sorting. In *Proc. CoLing/ACL*, pages 279–286. Association for Computational Linguistics.

Jonathan Graehl and Kevin Knight. 2004. Training tree transducers. In *HLT-NAACL*, pages 105–112. Association for Computational Linguistics. See also (Graehl et al., 2008).

Jonathan Graehl, Kevin Knight, and Jonathan May. 2008. Training tree transducers. *Computational Linguistics*, 34(3):391–427.

Kevin Knight. 2007. Capturing practical natural language transformations. *Machine Translation*, 21(2):121–133.

Zhifei Li and Jason Eisner. 2009. First- and second-order expectation semirings with applications to minimum-risk training on translation forests. In *Proc. EMNLP*, pages 40–51. Association for Computational Linguistics.

Eric Lilin. 1981. Propriétés de clôture d'une extension de transducteurs d'arbres déterministes. In *CAAP*, volume 112 of LNCS, pages 280–289. Springer.

Andreas Maletti, Jonathan Graehl, Mark Hopkins, and Kevin Knight. 2009. The power of extended top-down tree transducers. *SIAM J. Comput.*, 39(2):410–430.

Mark-Jan Nederhof and Giorgio Satta. 2003. Probabilistic parsing as intersection. In *Proc. IWPT*, pages 137–148. Association for Computational Linguistics.

Rebecca Nesson, Giorgio Satta, and Stuart M. Shieber. 2008. Optimal k-arization of synchronous tree-adjoining grammar. In *Proc. ACL*, pages 604–612. Association for Computational Linguistics.

Jacques Sakarovitch. 2009. Rational and recognisable power series. In Manfred Droste, Werner Kuich, and Heiko Vogler, editors, *Handbook of Weighted Automata*, EATCS Monographs on Theoret. Comput. Sci., chapter IV, pages 105–174. Springer.

Giorgio Satta and Enoch Peserico. 2005. Some computational complexity results for synchronous context-free grammars. In *Proc. HLT-EMNLP*, pages 803–810. Association for Computational Linguistics.

Marcel Paul Schützenberger. 1961. On the definition of a family of automata. *Information and Control*, 4(2–3):245–270.

Daniel H. Younger. 1967. Recognition and parsing of context-free languages in time n^3. *Inform. Control*, 10(2):189–208.

Hao Zhang, Liang Huang, Daniel Gildea, and Kevin Knight. 2006. Synchronous binarization for machine translation. In *Proc. HLT-NAACL*, pages 256–263. Association for Computational Linguistics.

Millstream Systems – a Formal Model for Linking Language Modules by Interfaces

Suna Bensch
Department of Computing Science,
Umeå University, Umeå, Sweden
suna@cs.umu.se

Frank Drewes
Department of Computing Science,
Umeå University, Umeå, Sweden
drewes@cs.umu.se

Abstract

We introduce Millstream systems, a formal model consisting of modules and an interface, where the modules formalise different aspects of language, and the interface links these aspects with each other.

1 Credits

This work is partially supported by the project *Tree Automata in Computational Language Technology* within the Sweden – South Africa Research Links Programme. A preliminary but more detailed version of this article is available as a technical report (Bensch and Drewes, 2009).

2 Introduction

Modern linguistic theories (Sadock, 1991; Jackendoff, 2002) promote the view that different aspects of language, such as phonology, morphology, syntax, and semantics should be viewed as autonomous modules that work simultaneously and are linked with each other by interfaces that describe their interaction and interdependency. Formalisms in modern computational linguistics which establish interfaces between different aspects of language are the Combinatory Categorical Grammar (CCG), the Functional Generative Description (FGD), the Head-Driven Phrase Structure Grammar (HPSG), the Lexical Functional Grammar (LFG), and the Extensible Dependency Grammar (XDG).[1] Here, we propose Millstream systems, an approach from a formal language theoretic point of view which is based on the same ideas as XDG, but uses tree-generating modules of arbitrary kinds.

Let us explain in slightly more detail what a Millstream system looks like. A Millstream system contains any number of tree generators, called its modules. Such a tree generator is any device that specifies a tree language. For example, a tree generator may be a context-free grammar, tree adjoining grammar, a finite-state tree automaton, a dependency grammar, a corpus, human input, etc. Even within a single Millstream system, the modules need not be of the same kind, since they are treated as "black boxes". The Millstream system links the trees generated by the modules by an interface consisting of logical formulas.

Suppose that a Millstream system has k modules. Then the interface consists of interface rules in the form of logical expressions that establish links between the (nodes of the) trees $t_1, \ldots, t_k$ that are generated by the individual modules. Thus, a valid combination of trees is not just any collection of trees $t_1, \ldots, t_k$ generated by the k modules. It also includes, between these structures, interconnecting links that represent their relationships and that must follow the rules expressed by the interface. Grammaticality, in terms of a Millstream system, means that the individual structures must be valid (i.e., generated by the modules) and are linked in such a way that all interface rules are logically satisfied. A Millstream system can thus be considered to perform independent concurrent derivations of autonomous modules, enriched by an interface that establishes links between the outputs of the modules, thus constraining the acceptable configurations.

Millstream systems may, for example, be of interest for natural language understanding and natural language generation. Simply put, the task of natural language understanding is to construct a suitable semantic representation of a sentence that has been heard (phonology) and parsed (syntax). Within the framework of Millstream systems this corresponds to the problem where we are given a syntactic tree (and possibly a phonological tree if such a module is involved) and the goal is to construct an appropriate semantic tree. Con-

[1]See, e.g., (Dalrymple, 2001; Sgall et al., 1986; Pollard and Sag, 1994; Steedman, 2000; Debusmann, 2006; Debusmann and Smolka, 2006).

Proceedings of the 2010 Workshop on Applications of Tree Automata in Natural Language Processing, ACL 2010, pages 28–36,
Uppsala, Sweden, 16 July 2010. ©2010 Association for Computational Linguistics

versely, natural language generation can be seen as the problem to construct an appropriate syntactic (and/or phonological) tree from a given semantic tree. In abstract terms, the situations just described are identical. We refer to the problem as the *completion problem*. While the current paper is mainly devoted to the introduction and motivation of Millstream systems, in (Bensch et al., 2010) the completion problem is investigated for so-called regular MSO Millstream systems, i.e. systems in which the modules are regular tree grammars (or, equivalently, finite tree automata) and the interface conditions are expressed in monadic second-order (MSO) logic. In Section 7, the results obtained so far are briefly summarised.

Now, let us roughly compare Millstream systems with XDG. Conceptually, the k modules of a Millstream system correspond to the k *dimensions* of an XDG. In an XDG, a configuration consists of dependency structures $t_1, \ldots, t_k$. The interface of a Millstream system corresponds to the *principles* of the XDG. The latter are logical formulas that express conditions that the collection of dependency structures must fulfill.

The major difference between the two formalisms lies in the fact that XDG inherently builds upon dependency structures, whereas the modules of a Millstream system are arbitrary tree generators. In XDG, each of $t_1, \ldots, t_k$ is a dependency analysis of the sentence considered. In particular, they share the yield and the set of nodes (as the nodes of a dependency tree correspond to the words in the sentence analysed, and its yield is that sentence). Millstream systems do not make similar assumptions, which means that they may give rise to new questions and possibilities:

- The purpose of a Millstream system is not necessarily the analysis of sentences. For example, a Millstream system with two modules could translate one language into another. For this, tree grammars representing the source and target languages could be used as modules, with an interface expressing that t_2 is a correct translation of t_1. This scenario makes no sense in the context of XDG, because the sentences represented by t_1 and t_2 differ. Many similar applications of Millstream system may the thought of, for example correction or simplification of sentences.
- As the modules may be arbitrary devices specifying tree languages, they contribute their own generative power and theoretical properties to the whole (in contrast to XDG, which does not have such a separation). This makes it possible to apply known results from tree language theory, and to study the interplay between different kinds of modules and interface logics.
- The fact that the individual modules of a Millstream system may belong to different classes of tree generators could be linguistically valuable. For example, a Millstream system combining a dependency grammar module with a regular tree grammar module, could be able to formalise aspects of a given natural language that cannot be formalised by using only one of these formalisms.
- For Millstream systems whose modules are generative grammar formalisms (such as regular tree grammars, tree-adjoining grammars and context-free tree grammars), it will be interesting to study conditions under which the Millstream system as a whole becomes generative, in the sense that well-formed configurations can be constructed in a step-by-step manner based on the derivation relations of the individual modules.

Let us finally mention another, somewhat subtle difference between XDG and Millstream systems. In XDG, the interfaces are dimensions on their own. For example, an XDG capturing the English syntax and semantics would have three dimensions, namely syntax, semantics, and the syntax-semantics interface. An analysis of a sentence would thus consist of three dependency trees, where the third one represents the relation between the other two. In contrast, a corresponding Millstream system would only have two modules. The interface between them is considered to be conceptually different and establishes direct links between the trees that are generated by the two modules. One of our tasks (which is, however, outside the scope of this contribution) is a study of the formal relation between XDG and Millstream systems, to achieve a proper understanding of their similarities and differences.

The rest of the paper is organised as follows. In the next section, we discuss an example illustrating the linguistic notions and ideas that Millstream systems attempt to provide a formal basis for. After some mathematical preliminaries, which are collected in Section 4, the formal definition of Millstream systems is presented in Section 5. Section 6 contains examples and remarks related to Formal Language Theory. Finally, Section 7 discusses preliminary results and future work.

3 Linguistical Background

In this section, we discuss an example, roughly following (Jackendoff, 2002), that illustrates the linguistic ideas that have motivated our approach. Figure 1 shows the phonological, syntactical and semantical structure, depicted as trees (a), (b) and (c), respectively of the sentence *Mary likes Peter*. Trees are defined formally in the next section, for the time being we assume the reader to be familiar with the general notion of a tree as used in linguistics and computer science.

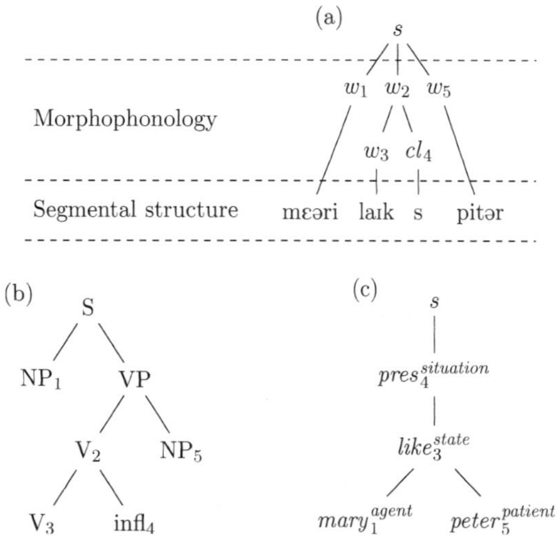

Figure 1: Phonological, syntactical and semantical structure of *Mary likes Peter*.

The segmental structure in the phonological tree (a) is the basic pronunciation of the sentence *Mary likes Peter*, where each symbol represents a speech sound. This string of speech sound symbols is structured into phonological words by morphophonolgy. The morphophonological structure in our example consists of the three full phonological words mɛəri, laɪk, pitər and of the clitic *s*. The clitic is attached to the adjacent phonological word, thus forming a larger phonological constituent. The syntactical tree (b) depicts the syntactical constituents. The sentence S is divided into a noun phrase NP and a verb phrase VP. The verb phrase VP is divided into an inflected verb V and a noun phrase NP. The inflected verb consists of its uninflected form and its inflection, which refers, in our example, to the grammatical features present tense and third person singular. The semantical tree (c) depicts the semantical constituents. In our example, $like$ is a function of type $state$ and takes two arguments, namely $mary$ and $peter$ which are of type $agent$ and $patient$.

The structure of *Mary likes Peter* is not just the sum of its phonological, syntactical and semantical structures. It also includes the relationships between certain constituents in these tree structures. To illustrate these relationships we use indices in Figure 1. The sole role of the indices here is to express the linguistic relationships among coindexed constituents. The indices do not occur in the formalisation, where they are replaced by logical links relating the nodes that, in the figure, carry the same indices.[2] The morphophonological word w_1, for example, is linked with the noun phrase NP_1 in the syntactical tree and with the conceptual constituent $mary_1^{agent}$ in the semantical tree. This illustrates that w_1, NP_1, and $mary_1^{agent}$ are the corresponding morphophonological, syntactical and semantical representations of *Mary*, respectively. But there are also correspondences that concern only the phonological and syntactical trees, excluding the semantical tree. For example, the inflected word V_2 in the syntactical structure corresponds to the phonological word w_2, but has no link to the semantical structure whatsoever.

4 Preliminaries

The set of non-negative integers is denoted by $\mathbb{N}$, and $\mathbb{N}_+ = \mathbb{N} \setminus \{0\}$. For $k \in \mathbb{N}$, we let $[k] = \{1, \ldots, k\}$. For a set S, the set of all nonempty finite sequences (or strings) over S is denoted by S^+; if the empty sequence ϵ is included, we write S^*. As usual, $A_1 \times \cdots \times A_k$ denotes the Cartesian product of sets $A_1, \ldots, A_k$. The transitive and reflexive closure of a binary relation $\Rightarrow \subseteq A \times A$ on a set A is denoted by $\Rightarrow^*$. A *ranked alphabet* is a finite set Σ of pairs (f, k), where f is a symbol and $k \in \mathbb{N}$ is its *rank*. We denote (f, k) by $f^{(k)}$, or simply by f if k is understood or of lesser importance. Further, we let $\Sigma^{(k)} = \{f^{(n)} \in \Sigma \mid n = k\}$. We define trees over Σ in one of the standard ways, by identifying the nodes of a tree t with sequences of natural numbers. Intuitively, such a sequence

[2]The reader is referred to (Bensch and Drewes, 2009) for the proper formalisation of the example in terms of a Millstream system.

shows that path from the root of the tree to the node in question. In particular, the root is the empty sequence ϵ.

Formally, the set T_Σ of trees over Σ consists of all mappings $t\colon V(t) \to \Sigma$ (called trees) with the following properties:

- The set $V(t)$ of *nodes of* t is a finite and non-empty prefix-closed subset of $\mathbb{N}_+^*$. Thus, for every node $vi \in V(t)$ (where $i \in \mathbb{N}_+$), its *parent* v is in $V(t)$ as well.
- For every node $v \in V(t)$, if $t(v) = f^{(k)}$, then $\{i \in \mathbb{N} \mid vi \in V(t)\} = [k]$. In other words, the *children* of v are $v1, \ldots, vk$.

Let $t \in \mathrm{T}_\Sigma$ be a tree. The *root* of t is the node ϵ. For every node $v \in V(t)$, the *subtree of t rooted at v* is denoted by t/v. It is defined by $V(t/v) = \{v' \in \mathbb{N}^* \mid vv' \in V(t)\}$ and, for all $v' \in V(t/v)$, $(t/v)(v') = t(vv')$. We shall denote a tree t as $f[t_1, \ldots, t_k]$ if $t(\epsilon) = f^{(k)}$ and $t/i = t_i$ for $i \in [k]$. In the special case where $k = 0$ (i.e., $V(t) = \{\epsilon\}$), the brackets may be omitted, thus denoting t as f. For a set S of trees, the set of all trees of the form $f[t_1, \ldots, t_k]$ such that $f^{(k)} \in \Sigma$ and $t_1, \ldots, t_k \in S$ is denoted by $\Sigma(S)$. For a tuple $T \in \mathrm{T}_\Sigma^k$, we let $V(T)$ denote the set $\{(i, v) \mid i \in [k] \text{ and } v \in V(t_i)\}$. Thus, $V(T)$ is the disjoint union of the sets $V(t_i)$. Furthermore, we let $V(T, i)$ denote the ith component of this disjoint union, i.e., $V(T, i) = \{i\} \times V(t_i)$ for all $i \in [k]$. A *tree language* is a subset of T_Σ, for a ranked alphabet Σ, and a *Σ-tree generator* (or simply *tree generator*) is any sort of formal device G that determines a tree language $L(G) \subseteq \mathrm{T}_\Sigma$. A typical sort of tree generator, which we will use in our examples, is the regular tree grammar.

Definition 1 (regular tree grammar). A *regular tree grammar* is a tuple $G = (N, \Sigma, R, S)$ consisting of disjoint ranked alphabets N and Σ of *nonterminals* and *terminals*, where $N = N^{(0)}$, a finite set R of rules $A \to r$, where $A \in N$ and $r \in \mathrm{T}_{\Sigma \cup N}$, and an *initial nonterminal* $S \in N$.

Given trees $t, t' \in \mathrm{T}_{\Sigma \cup N}$, there is a *derivation step* $t \Rightarrow t'$ if t' is obtained from t by replacing a single occurrence of a nonterminal A with r, where $A \to r$ is a rule in R. The *regular tree language generated by* G is

$$L(G) = \{t \in \mathrm{T}_\Sigma \mid S \overset{*}{\Rightarrow} t\}.$$

It is well known that a string language L is context-free if and only if there is a regular tree language L', such that $L = \mathrm{yield}(L')$. Here, $\mathrm{yield}(L') = \{\mathrm{yield}(t) \mid t \in L'\}$ denotes the set of all yields of trees in L', the yield $\mathrm{yield}(t)$ of a tree t being the string obtained by reading its leaves from left to right.

5 Millstream Systems

Throughout the rest of this paper, let Λ denote any type of predicate logic that allows us to make use of n-ary predicates symbols. We indicate the arity of predicate symbols in the same way as the rank of symbols in ranked alphabets, i.e., by writing $P^{(n)}$ if P is a predicate symbol of arity n. The set of all well-formed formulas in Λ without free variables (i.e., the set of sentences of Λ) is denoted by F_Λ. If S is a set, we say that a predicate symbol $P^{(n)}$ is S-typed if it comes with an associated type $(s_1, \ldots, s_n) \in S^n$. We write $P\colon s_1 \times \cdots \times s_n$ to specify the type of P. Recall that an n-ary predicate ψ on D is a function $\psi\colon D^n \to \{\mathrm{true}, \mathrm{false}\}$. Alternatively, ψ can be viewed as a subset of D^n, namely the set of all $(d_1, \ldots, d_n) \in D^n$ such that $\psi(d_1, \ldots, d_n) = \mathrm{true}$. We use these views interchangeably, selecting whichever is more convenient. Given a (finite) set $\mathcal{P}$ of predicate symbols, a logical structure $\langle D; (\psi_P)_{P \in \mathcal{P}} \rangle$ consists of a set D called the domain and, for each $P^{(n)} \in \mathcal{P}$, a predicate $\psi_P \subseteq D^n$. If an existing structure Z is enriched with additional predicates $(\psi_P)_{P \in \mathcal{P}'}$ (where $\mathcal{P} \cap \mathcal{P}' = \emptyset$), we denote the resulting structure by $\langle Z; (\psi_P)_{P \in \mathcal{P}'} \rangle$. In this paper, we will only consider structures with finite domains. To represent (tuples of) trees as logical structures, consider a ranked alphabet Σ, and let r be the maximum rank of symbols in Σ. A tuple $T = (t_1, \ldots, t_k) \in \mathrm{T}_\Sigma^k$ will be represented by the structure

$$|T| = \langle V(T); (V_i)_{i \in [k]}, (\mathrm{lab}_g)_{g \in \Sigma}, (\downarrow_i)_{i \in [r]} \rangle$$

consisting of the domain $V(T)$ and the predicates $V_i^{(1)}$ ($i \in [k]$), $\mathrm{lab}_g^{(1)}$ ($g \in \Sigma$) and $\downarrow_i^{(2)}$ ($i \in [r]$). The predicates are given as follows:

- For every $i \in [k]$, $V_i = V(T, i)$. Thus, $V_i(d)$ expresses that d is a node in t_i (or, to be precise, that d represents a node of t_i in the disjoint union $V(T)$).
- For every $g \in \Sigma$, $\mathrm{lab}_g = \{(i, v) \in V(T) \mid i \in [k] \text{ and } t_i(v) = g\}$. Thus, $\mathrm{lab}_g(d)$ expresses that the label of d is g.
- For every $j \in [r]$, $\downarrow_j = \{((i, v), (i, vj)) \mid i \in [k] \text{ and } v, vj \in V(t_i)\}$. Thus, $\downarrow_j(d, d')$

expresses that d' is the jth child of d in one of the trees $t_1, \ldots, t_k$. In the following, we write $d \downarrow_j d'$ instead of $\downarrow_j(d, d')$.

Note that, in the definition of $|T|$, we have blurred the distinction between predicate symbols and their interpretation as predicates, because this interpretation is fixed. Especially in intuitive explanations, we shall sometimes also identify the logical structure $|T|$ with the tuple T it represents.

To define Millstream systems, we start by formalising our notion of interfaces. The idea is that a tuple $T = (t_1, \ldots, t_k)$ of trees, represented by the structure $|T|$, is augmented with additional *interface links* that are subject to logical conditions. An interface may contain finitely many different kinds of interface links. Formally, the collection of all interface links of a given kind is viewed as a logical predicate. The names of the predicates are called interface symbols. Each interface symbol is given a type that indicates which trees it is intended to link with each other.

For example, if we want to make use of ternary links called TIE, each linking a node of t_1 with a node of t_3 and a node of t_4, we use the interface symbol $\text{TIE}\colon 1 \times 3 \times 4$. This interface symbol would then be interpreted as a predicate $\psi_{\text{TIE}} \subseteq V(T,1) \times V(T,3) \times V(T,4)$. Each triple in ψ_{TIE} would thus be an interface link of type TIE that links a node in $V(t_1)$ with a node in $V(t_3)$ and a node in $V(t_4)$.

Definition 2 (interface)**.** Let Σ be a ranked alphabet. An *interface on* T_Σ^k *(*$k \in \mathbb{N}$*)* is a pair $\mathit{INT} = (\mathcal{I}, \Phi)$, such that

- $\mathcal{I}$ is a finite set of $[k]$-typed predicate symbols called *interface symbols*, and
- Φ is a finite set of formulas in F_Λ that may, in addition to the fixed vocabulary of Λ, contain the predicate symbols in $\mathcal{I}$ and those of the structures $|T|$ (where $T \in \mathrm{T}_\Sigma^k$). These formulas are called *interface conditions*.

A *configuration* (w.r.t. INT) is a structure $C = \langle |T|; (\psi_I)_{I \in \mathcal{I}} \rangle$, such that

- $T \subseteq \mathrm{T}_\Sigma^k$,
- $\psi_I \subseteq V(T, i_1) \times \cdots \times V(T, i_l)$ for every interface symbol $I\colon i_1 \times \cdots \times i_l$ in $\mathcal{I}$, and
- C satisfies the interface conditions in Φ (if each symbol $I \in \mathcal{I}$ is interpreted as ψ_I).

Note that several interfaces can always be combined into one by just taking the union of their sets of interface symbols and interface conditions.

Definition 3 (Millstream system)**.** Let Σ be a ranked alphabet and $k \in \mathbb{N}$. A *Millstream system* (MS, for short) is a system of the form $\mathit{MS} = (M_1, \ldots, M_k; \mathit{INT})$ consisting of Σ-tree generators $M_1, \ldots, M_k$, called the *modules* of MS, and an interface INT on T_Σ^k. The language $L(\mathit{MS})$ generated by MS is the set of all configurations $\langle |T|; (\psi_I)_{I \in \mathcal{I}} \rangle$ such that $T \in L(M_1) \times \cdots \times L(M_k)$.

Sometimes we consider only some of the trees in these tuples. For this, if MS is as above and $1 \le i_1 < \cdots < i_l \le k$, we define the notation

$$L^{M_{i_1} \times \cdots \times M_{i_l}}(\mathit{MS}) = \{(t_{i_1}, \ldots, t_{i_l}) \mid \langle |(t_1, \ldots, t_k); (\psi_I)_{I \in \mathcal{I}}| \rangle \in L(\mathit{MS})\}.$$

The reader should note that, intentionally, Millstream systems are not a priori "generative". Even less so, they are "derivational" by nature. This is because there is no predefined notion of derivation that allows us to create configurations by means of a stepwise (though typically nondeterministic) procedure. In fact, there cannot be one, unless we make specific assumptions regarding the way in which the modules work, but also regarding the logic Λ and the form of the interface conditions that may be used. Similarly, as mentioned in the introduction, there is no predefined order of importance or priority among the modules.

6 Examples and Remarks Related to Formal Language Theory

The purpose of this section is to indicate, by means of examples and easy observations, that Millstream systems are not only linguistically well motivated, but also worth studying from the point of view of computer science, most notably regarding their algorithmic and language-theoretic properties. While this kind of study is beyond the scope of the current article, part of our future research on Millstream systems will be devoted to such questions.

Example 1. Let Λ be ordinary first-order logic with equality, and consider the Millstream system MS over $\Sigma = \{\circ^{(2)}, a^{(0)}, b^{(0)}, c^{(0)}, d^{(0)}\}$ which consists of two identical modules $M_1 = M_2$ that simply generate T_Σ (e.g., using the regular tree grammar with the single nonterminal S and the rules[3] $S \rightarrow \circ[S,S] \mid a \mid b \mid c \mid d$) and a single interface symbol BIJ: 1×2 with the interface conditions

$$\forall x\colon \mathrm{lab}_{\{a,b,c,d\}}(x) \leftrightarrow \exists y\colon \mathrm{BIJ}(x,y) \vee \mathrm{BIJ}(y,x),$$
$$\forall x,y,z\colon (\mathrm{BIJ}(x,y) \wedge \mathrm{BIJ}(x,z) \vee \mathrm{BIJ}(y,x) \wedge \mathrm{BIJ}(z,x)) \rightarrow y = z,$$
$$\forall x,y\colon \mathrm{BIJ}(x,y) \rightarrow \bigvee_{z\in\{a,b,c,d\}} (\mathrm{lab}_z(x) \wedge \mathrm{lab}_z(y)).$$

The first interface condition expresses that all and only the leaves of both trees are linked. The second expresses that no leaf is linked with two or more leaves. In effect, this amounts to saying that BIJ is a bijection between the leaves of the two trees. The third interface condition expresses that this bijection is label preserving. Altogether, this amounts to saying that the yields of the two trees are permutations of each other; see Figure 2.

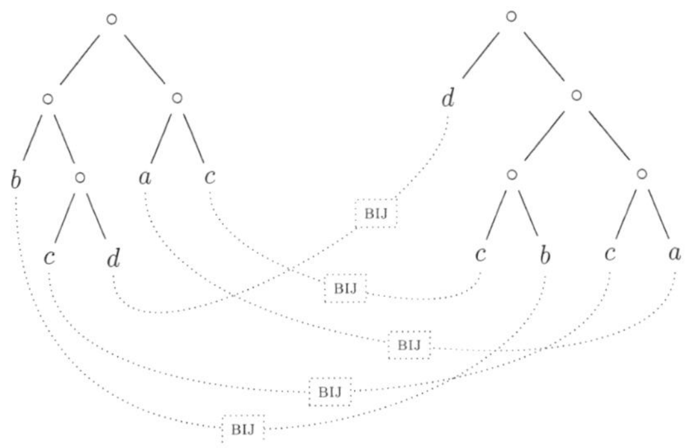

Figure 2: An element of $L(MS)$ in Example 1.

Now, let us replace the modules by slightly more interesting ones. For a string w over $\{A,B,a,b,c,d\}$, let $\underline{w}$ denote any tree over $\{\circ^{(2)}, A^{(0)}, B^{(0)}, a^{(0)}, b^{(0)}, c^{(0)}, d^{(0)}\}$ with $\mathrm{yield}(\underline{w}) = w$. (For example, we may choose $\underline{w}$ to be the left comb whose leaf symbols are given by w.) Let the Millstream system MS' be defined as MS, but using the modules $M_1' = (\{A,B,C,D\},\Sigma,R_1,A)$ and $M_2' = (\{A,B\},\Sigma,R_2,A)$ with the following rules:

$$R_1' = \{A \rightarrow \underline{aA} \mid \underline{aB},\ B \rightarrow \underline{bB} \mid \underline{bC},\ C \rightarrow \underline{cC} \mid \underline{cD},\ D \rightarrow \underline{dD} \mid \underline{d}\},$$
$$R_2' = \{A \rightarrow \underline{acA} \mid \underline{acB},\ B \rightarrow \underline{bdB} \mid \underline{bd}\}.$$

Thus, M_1' and M_2' are the "standard" grammars (written as regular tree grammars) that generate the regular languages $\{a^k b^l c^m d^n \mid k,l,m,n \geq 1\}$ and $\{(ac)^m (bd)^n \mid m,n \geq 1\}$. The interface makes sure that $L^{M_1' \times M_2'}(MS')$ contains only those pairs of trees t_1, t_2 in which $\mathrm{yield}(t_1)$ is a permutation of $\mathrm{yield}(t_2)$. As a consequence, it follows that $\mathrm{yield}(L^{M_1'}(MS)) = \{a^m b^n c^m d^n \mid m,n \geq 1\}$.

[3] As usual, $A \rightarrow r \mid r'$ stands for $A \rightarrow r$, $A \rightarrow r'$.

The next example discusses how top-down tree transductions can be implemented as Millstream systems.

Example 2 (top-down tree transduction). Recall that a *tree transduction* is a binary relation $\tau \subseteq \mathrm{T}_\Sigma \times \mathrm{T}_{\Sigma'}$, where Σ and Σ' are ranked alphabets. The set of trees that a tree $t \in \mathrm{T}_\Sigma$ is transformed into is given by $\tau(t) = \{t' \in \mathrm{T}_{\Sigma'} \mid (t,t') \in \tau\}$. Obviously, every Millstream system of the form $MS = (M_1, M_2; INT)$ defines a tree transduction, namely $L^{M_1 \times M_2}(MS)$. Let us consider a very simple instance of a deterministic top-down tree transduction τ (see, e.g., (Gécseg and Steinby, 1997; Fülöp and Vogler, 1998; Comon et al., 2007) for definitions and references regarding top-down tree transductions), where $\Sigma = \Sigma' = \{f^{(2)}, g^{(2)}, a^{(0)}\}$. We transform a tree $t \in \mathrm{T}_\Sigma$ into the tree obtained from t by interchanging the subtrees of all top-most fs (i.e., of all nodes that are labelled with f and do not have an ancestor that is labelled with f as well) and turning the f at hand into a g. To accomplish this, a top-down tree transducer would use two states, say SWAP and COPY, to traverse the input tree from the top down, starting in state SWAP. Whenever an f is reached in this state, its subtrees are interchanged and the traversal continues in parallel on each of the subtrees in state COPY. The only purpose of this state is to copy the input to the output without changing it. Formally, this would be expressed by the following term rewrite rules, viewing the states as symbols of rank 1:

$$\begin{aligned}
\mathrm{SWAP}[f[x_1,x_2]] &\rightarrow g[\mathrm{COPY}[x_2], \mathrm{COPY}[x_1]],\\
\mathrm{COPY}[f[x_1,x_2]] &\rightarrow f[\mathrm{COPY}[x_1], \mathrm{COPY}[x_2]],\\
\mathrm{SWAP}[g[x_1,x_2]] &\rightarrow g[\mathrm{SWAP}[x_1], \mathrm{SWAP}[x_2]],\\
\mathrm{COPY}[g[x_1,x_2]] &\rightarrow g[\mathrm{COPY}[x_1], \mathrm{COPY}[x_2]],\\
\mathrm{SWAP}[a] &\rightarrow a,\\
\mathrm{COPY}[a] &\rightarrow a.
\end{aligned}$$

(We hope that these rules are intuitive enough to be understood even by readers who are unfamiliar with top-down tree transducers, as giving the formal definition of top-down tree transducers would be out of the scope of this article.) We mimic the behaviour of the top-down tree transducer using a Millstream system with interface symbols SWAP: 1×2 and COPY: 1×2. Since the modules simply generate T_Σ, they are not explicitly discussed. The idea behind the interface is that an interface link labelled $q \in \{\text{SWAP}, \text{COPY}\}$ links a node v in the input tree with a node v' in the output tree if the simulated computation of the tree transducer reaches v in state q, resulting in node v' in the output tree. First, we specify that the initial state is SWAP, which simply means that the roots of the two trees are linked by a SWAP link:

$$\forall x, y\colon root_1(x) \wedge root_2(y) \rightarrow \text{SWAP}(x, y),$$

where $root_i$ is defined as $root_i(x) \equiv V_i(x) \wedge \nexists y\colon y \downarrow_1 x$. It expresses that x is the root of tree i. The next interface condition corresponds to the first rule of the simulated top-down tree transducer:

$$\forall x, y, x_1, x_2\colon \text{SWAP}(x, y) \wedge \text{lab}_f(x) \wedge x \downarrow_1 x_1 \wedge x \downarrow_2 x_2 \rightarrow \text{lab}_g(y) \wedge \exists y_1, y_2\colon y \downarrow_1 y_1 \wedge y \downarrow_2 y_2 \wedge \text{COPY}(x_1, y_2) \wedge \text{COPY}(x_2, y_1).$$

In a similar way, the remaining rules are turned into interface conditions, e.g.,

$$\forall x, y, x_1, x_2\colon \text{COPY}(x, y) \wedge \text{lab}_f(x) \wedge x \downarrow_1 x_1 \wedge x \downarrow_2 x_2 \rightarrow \text{lab}_f(y) \wedge \exists y_1, y_2\colon y \downarrow_1 y_1 \wedge y \downarrow_2 y_2 \wedge \text{COPY}(x_1, y_1) \wedge \text{COPY}(x_2, y_2).$$

The reader should easily be able to figure out the remaining interface conditions required.

One of the elements of $L(MS)$ is shown in Figure 3. It should not be difficult to see that, indeed, $L^{M_1 \times M_2}(MS) = \tau$.

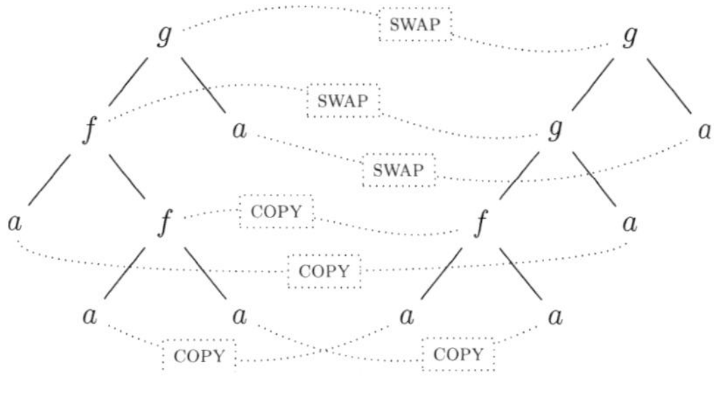

Figure 3: An element of $L(MS)$ in Example 2.

Extending the previous example, one can easily see that all top-down and bottom-up tree transductions can be turned into Millstream systems in a way similar to the construction above. A similar remark holds for many other types of tree transductions known from the literature. Most notably, monadic second-order definable tree transductions (Engelfriet and Maneth, 1999; Engelfriet and Hoogeboom, 2001; Engelfriet and Maneth, 2003) can be expressed as Millstream systems. Since the mentioned types of tree transductions are well studied, and much is known about their algorithmic properties, future research on Millstream systems should investigate the relationship between different types of tree transductions and Millstream systems in detail. In particular, it should be tried to formulate requirements on the interface conditions that can be used to obtain characterisations of various classes of tree transductions. We note here that results of this type would not only be interesting from a purely mathematical point of view, since tree transducers have turned out to be a valuable tool in, for example, machine translation (Knight and Graehl, 2005; May and Knight, 2006; Graehl et al., 2008).

7 Preliminary Results and Future Work

Millstream systems, as introduced in this article, are formal devices that allow to model situations in which several tree-generating modules are interconnected by logical interfaces. In a forthcoming paper (Bensch et al., 2010), we investigate the theoretical properties of regular MSO Millstream systems, i.e., Millstream systems in which the modules are regular tree grammars and the logic used is monadic second-order logic. In particular, we study the so-called *completion problem.* Given a Millstream system with k modules and $l \leq k$ *known trees* $t_{i_1}, \ldots, t_{i_l}$ $(1 \leq i_1 < \cdots < i_l \leq k)$, the task is to find a *completion*, i.e., a configuration whose i_jth tree is t_{i_j} for all $j \in [l]$. Thus, if viewed as a pure decision problem, the completion problem corresponds to the membership problem for $L^{M_{i_1} \times \cdots \times M_{i_l}}(MS)$. To be useful in applications, algorithms solving the completion problem should, of course, be required to explicitly construct a completion rather than just answering *yes*.

Let us briefly summarize the results of (Bensch et al., 2010).

1. In general, the completion problem is undecidable for $k - l \geq 2$ even in the case where only the use of first-order logic is permitted. This can be shown by reducing Post's correspondence problem (PCP) to the emptiness problem for a regular FO Millstream system with $k = 2$. The Millstream system constructed is somewhat similar to the one in Example 1, as it establishes bijective correspondences between the nodes of two trees (that

represent the two parts of a solution to a PCP instance).

2. If there are no direct links between unknown trees (i.e., $|\{j_1, \ldots, j_m\} \setminus \{i_1, \ldots, i_l\}| \leq 1$ for each interface symbol $I\colon j_1 \times \cdots \times j_m$), then the completion problem is solvable for all regular MSO Millstream systems.

3. Applying some well-known results, the completion problem is solvable for all regular MSO Millstream systems for which $L(MS)$ is of bounded tree width. Thus, it is of interest to establish conditions that guarantee the configurations in $L(MS)$ to be of bounded tree width. Two such conditions, are given in (Bensch et al., 2010). Roughly speaking, they require that the links respect the structure of the trees. Let us informally describe one of them, called nestedness. Say that a link $I'(u_1, \ldots, u_m)$ is *directly below* a link $I(v_1, \ldots, v_l)$ if there are i, j such that u_j is a descendant of v_i and none of the nodes in between carries a link. Now, fix a constant h. A configuration is *nested* if the roots are linked with each other and the following hold for every link $\lambda = I(v_1, \ldots, v_l)$:

   (a) There are at most h links $I'(u_1, \ldots, u_m)$ directly below λ.

   (b) Each of the nodes u_j in (a) is a descendant of one of the nodes v_i.

   As mentioned above, $L(MS)$ is of bounded tree width if its configurations are nested (with respect to the same constant h).

Nestedness, and also the second sufficient condition for bounded tree width studied in (Bensch et al., 2010) restrict the configurations themselves. While such conditions may be appropriate in many practical cases (where one *knows* what the configurations look like), future research should also attempt to find out whether it is possible to put some easily testable requirements on the interface conditions in order to force the configurations to be of bounded tree width. Note that, since the property of being of tree width at most d is expressible in monadic second-order logic, one can always artificially force the configurations of a given MSO Millstream system to be of bounded tree width, but this is not very useful as it would simply exclude those configurations whose tree width is greater than the desired constant d, thus changing the semantics of the given Millstream system in a usually undesired manner.

Future work should also investigate properties that make it possible to obtain or complete configurations in a generative way. For example, for regular MSO Millstream systems with interface conditions of a suitable type, it should be possible to generate the configurations in $L(MS)$ by generating the k trees in a parallel top-down manner, at the same time establishing the interface links. Results of this kind could also be used for solving the completion problem in an efficient manner. In general, it is clear that efficiency must be an important aspect of future theoretical investigations into Millstream systems.

In addition to theoretical results, a good implementation of Millstream systems is needed in order to make it possible to implement nontrivial examples. While this work should, to the extent possible, be application independent, it will also be necessary to seriously attempt to formalise and implement linguistic theories as Millstream systems. This includes exploring various such theories with respect to their appropriateness.

To gain further insight into the usefulness and limitations of Millstream systems for Computational Linguistics, future work should elaborate if and how it is possible to translate formalisms such as HPSG, LFG, CCG, FDG and XDG into Millstream systems.

Acknowledgments

We thank Dot and Danie van der Walt for providing us with a calm and relaxed atmosphere at Millstream Guest House in Stellenbosch (South Africa), where the first ideas around Millstream systems were born in April 2009. Scientifically, we would like to thank Henrik Björklund, Stephen J. Hegner, and Brink van der Merwe for discussions and constructive input. Furthermore, we would like to thank one of the referees for valuable comments.

References

Suna Bensch and Frank Drewes. 2009. Millstream systems. Report UMINF 09.21, Umeå University. Available at `http://www8.cs.umu.se/research/uminf/index.cgi?year=2009&number=21`.

Suna Bensch, Henrik Björklund, and Frank Drewes. 2010. Algorithmic properties of Millstream systems. In Sheng Yu, editor, *Proc. 14th Intl. Conf. on Developments in Language Theory (DLT 2010)*, Lecture Notes in Computer Science. To appear.

Hubert Comon, Max Dauchet, Rémi Gilleron, Florent Jacquemard, Christof Löding, Denis Lugiez, Sophie Tison, and Marc Tommasi. 2007. *Tree Automata Techniques and Applications*. Internet publication available at `http://tata.gforge.inria.fr`. Release October 2007.

Mary Dalrymple. 2001. *Lexical Functional Grammar*, volume 34 of *Syntax and Semantics*. Academic Press.

Ralph Debusmann and Gert Smolka. 2006. Multi-dimensional dependency grammar as multigraph description. In *Proceedings of FLAIRS Conference*, pages 740–745.

Ralph Debusmann. 2006. *Extensible Dependency Grammar: A Modular Grammar Formalism Based On Multigraph Description*. Ph.D. thesis, Universität des Saarlandes. Available at `http://www.ps.uni-sb.de/~rade/papers/diss.pdf`.

Joost Engelfriet and Henrik Jan Hoogeboom. 2001. MSO definable string transductions and two-way finite-state transducers. *ACM Transactions on Computational Logic*, 2:216–254.

Joost Engelfriet and Sebastian Maneth. 1999. Macro tree transducers, attribute grammars, and MSO definable tree translations. *Information and Computation*, 154:34–91.

Joost Engelfriet and Sebastian Maneth. 2003. Macro tree translations of linear size increase are MSO definable. *SIAM Journal on Computing*, 32:950–1006.

Zoltán Fülöp and Heiko Vogler. 1998. *Syntax-Directed Semantics: Formal Models Based on Tree Transducers*. Springer.

Ferenc Gécseg and Magnus Steinby. 1997. Tree languages. In G. Rozenberg and A. Salomaa, editors, *Handbook of Formal Languages. Vol. 3: Beyond Words*, chapter 1, pages 1–68. Springer.

Jonathan Graehl, Kevin Knight, and Jonathan May. 2008. Training tree transducers. *Computational Linguistics*, 34(3):391–427.

Ray Jackendoff. 2002. *Foundations of Language: Brain, Meaning, Grammar, Evolution*. Oxford University Press, Oxford.

Kevin Knight and Jonathan Graehl. 2005. An overview of probabilistic tree transducers for natural language processing. In Alexander F. Gelbukh, editor, *Proc. 6th Intl. Conf. on Computational Linguistics and Intelligent Text Processing (CICLing 2005)*, volume 3406 of Lecture Notes in Computer Science, pages 1–24. Springer.

Jonathan May and Kevin Knight. 2006. Tiburon: A weighted tree automata toolkit. In Oscar H. Ibarra and Hsu-Chun Yen, editors, *Proc. 11th Intl. Conf. on Implementation and Application of Automata (CIAA 2006)*, volume 4094 of Lecture Notes in Computer Science, pages 102–113. Springer.

Carl Pollard and Ivan Sag. 1994. *Head-Driven Phrase Structure Grammar*. Chicago University Press.

Jerrold Sadock. 1991. *Autolexical Syntax - A Theory of Parallel Grammatical Representations*. The University of Chicago Press, Chicago & London.

Petr Sgall, Eva Hajičová, and Jarmila Panevová. 1986. *The meaning of the sentence in its semantic and pragmatic aspects*. Reidel, Dordrecht.

Mark Steedman. 2000. *The Syntactic Process (Language, Speech, and Communication)*. MIT Press.

Transforming Lexica as Trees

Mark-Jan Nederhof
University of St Andrews
North Haugh, St Andrews
KY16 9SX
Scotland

Abstract

We investigate the problem of structurally changing lexica, while preserving the information. We present a type of lexicon transformation that is complete on an interesting class of lexica. Our work is motivated by the problem of merging one or more lexica into one lexicon. Lexica, lexicon schemas, and lexicon transformations are all seen as particular kinds of trees.

1 Introduction

A standard for lexical resources, called Lexical Markup Framework (LMF), has been developed under the auspices of ISO (Francopoulo et al., 2006). At its core is the understanding that most information represented in a lexicon is hierarchical in nature, so that it can be represented as a tree. Although LMF also includes relations between nodes orthogonal to the tree structure, we will in this paper simplify the presentation by treating only purely tree-shaped lexica.

There is a high demand for tools supporting the merger of a number of lexica. A few examples of papers that express this demand are Chan Ka-Leung and Wu (1999), Jing et al. (2000), Monachini et al. (2004) and Ruimy (2006). A typical scenario is the following. The ultimate goal of a project is the creation of a single lexicon for a given language. In order to obtain the necessary data, several field linguists independently gather lexical resources. Despite efforts to come to agreements before the start of the field work, there will generally be overlap in the scope of the respective resources and there are frequently inconsistencies both in the lexical information itself and in the form in which information is represented. In the latter case, the information needs to be restructured as part of the process of creating a single lexicon.

We have developed a model of the merging process, and experiments with an implementation are underway. The actions performed by the tool are guided by a linguist, but portions of the work may also be done purely mechanically, if this is so specified by the user. The purpose of the present paper is to study one aspect of the adequacy of the model, namely the restructuring of information, with one input lexicon and one output lexicon. This corresponds to a special use of our tool, which may in general produce one output lexicon out of any number of input lexica.

As our lexica are trees, the use of well-established techniques such as term unification (Lloyd, 1984) and tree transduction (Fülöp and Vogler, 1998) seem obvious candidates for solutions to our problem. Also technologies such as XSL (Harold and Means, 2004) and XQuery (Walmsley, 2007) spring to mind. We have chosen a different approach however, which, as we will show, has favourable theoretical properties.

The structure of this paper is as follows. The type of lexicon that we consider is formalized in Section 2, and lexicon transformations are discussed in Section 3. Section 4 shows that the proposed type of lexicon transformation suffices to map all 'reasonable' lexica to one another, as long as they contain the same information. Conditions under which transformations preserve information are discussed in Section 5. A brief overview of an implementation is given in Section 6.

2 Lexica and their structures

In this section, we formalize the notions of lexica, lexicon structures, and their meanings, abstracting

Proceedings of the 2010 Workshop on Applications of Tree Automata in Natural Language Processing, ACL 2010, pages 37–45,
Uppsala, Sweden, 16 July 2010.

away from details that are irrelevant to the discussion that follows.

A *lexicon schema* S is a tuple (A, C, T), where A is a finite set of *attributes*, C is a finite set of *components* ($A \cap C = \emptyset$), and T is a labelled, unordered tree such that:

- each leaf node is labelled by an element from A,
- each non-leaf node is labelled by an element from C, and
- each element from $A \cup C$ occurs exactly once.

A *lexicon* L is a tuple (A, V, C, t), where A is as above, V is a set of *values*, C is as above, and t is a labelled, unordered tree such that:

- each leaf node is labelled by an element from $A \times V$,
- each non-leaf node is labelled by an element from C,
- if a leaf node with a label of the form (a, v_1) has a parent labelled c, then *each* leaf node with a label of the form (a, v_2) has a parent labelled c, and
- if a non-leaf node labelled c_1 has a parent labelled c_2, then *each* non-leaf node labelled c_1 has a parent labelled c_2.

Due to the last two constraints, we may compare lexica and lexicon schemata. In order to simplify this comparison, we will assume that in a lexicon, A and C only contain elements that occur in t. This is without loss of generality, as unused elements of A and C can be omitted. We will also assume that t contains at least two nodes, so that the root is not a leaf.

We say a lexicon $L = (A_L, V, C_L, t)$ is an *instance* of lexicon schema $S = (A_S, C_S, T)$ if $A_L \subseteq A_S$, $C_L \subseteq C_S$, and furthermore:

- the label of the root of t equals the label of the root of T,
- if a leaf node of t with a label of the form (a, v_1) has a parent labelled c, then the leaf node of T labelled a has a parent labelled c, and
- if a non-leaf node of t labelled c_1 has a parent labelled c_2, then the non-leaf node of T labelled c_1 has a parent labelled c_2.

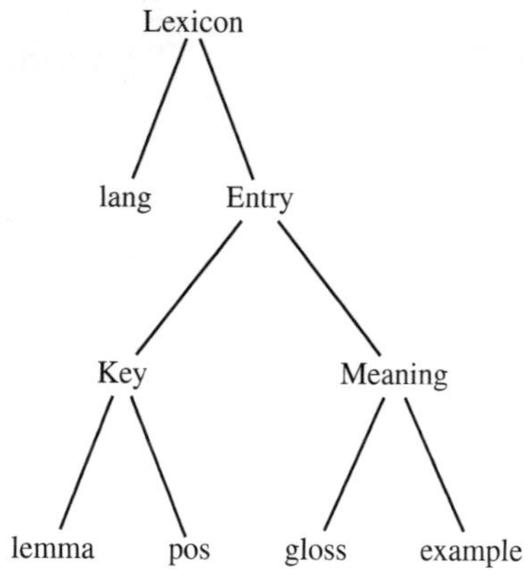

Figure 1: A lexicon schema S.

Examples of a lexicon schema and a lexicon are given in Figures 1 and 2. For the sake of succinctness, an attribute-value pair such as (example, 'Er ist mit dem Zug gefahren') is commonly separated by $=$, and where it is required for graphical reasons, the value may be drawn beneath the attribute, stretched out vertically.

On a number of occasions in the constructions and proofs that follow, it is convenient to assume that the root node of a lexicon schema has exactly one child. If this does not hold, as in the running example, we may introduce an artificial root node labelled by an artificial component, denoted by '\$', which has the conceptual root node as only child. We will refer to the lexicon schema that results as an *extended* lexicon schema. (Cf. the theory of context-free grammars, which are often extended with a new start symbol.) As a consequence, a lexicon that is an instance of an extended lexicon schema may, in pathological cases, have several nodes that are labelled by the conceptual root component of the schema.

The components in lexicon schemata and lexica provide a means of structuring sets of attributes, or sets of attribute-value pairs respectively, into tree-shaped forms. The discussion that follows will treat components and structure as secondary, and will take attributes and attribute-value pairs as the primary carriers of information.

A *lexicon base* B is a tuple (A, V, I), where A and V are as above, and I is a finite non-empty set of *items*, each of which is a partial function from A to V, defined on at least one attribute. Such partial functions will also be represented as non-empty sets of attribute-value pairs, in which each attribute occurs at most once.

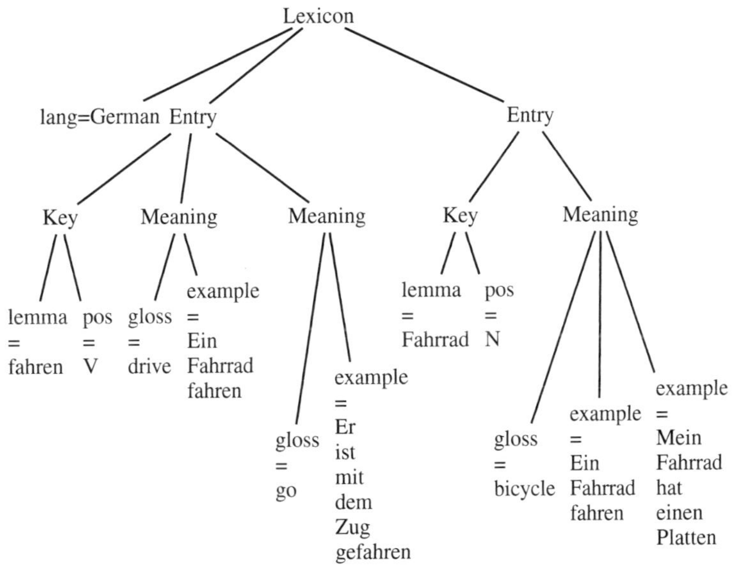

Figure 2: A lexicon L that is an instance of S from Figure 1.

Let $L = (A, V, C, t)$ be a lexicon, where r is the root of t. Its base, denoted by $B(L)$, is (A, V, I) with $I = I(r)$, where the function I on nodes n of the lexicon is defined as follows.

- For a leaf node n labelled by the attribute-value pair (a, v), $I(n) = \{\{(a, v)\}\}$. In words, the set $I(n)$ contains only one item, which is a partial function mapping attribute a to value v.

- For a non-leaf node n, assume that m different components or attributes $d_1, \ldots, d_m$ occur among the children. (Each element d is either a component or an attribute.) Let N_j $(1 \leq j \leq m)$ be the set of children of n labelled by d_j if d_j is a component or by (d_j, v), some value v, if d_j is an attribute. Then:

$$I(n) = \{\iota_1 \cup \cdots \cup \iota_m \mid n_1 \in N_1, \ldots, n_m \in N_m, \iota_1 \in I(n_1), \ldots, \iota_m \in I(n_m)\}.$$

Note that by the definition of lexica and of $N_1, \ldots, N_m$, no attribute may occur both in ι_i and in ι_j if $i \neq j$. This means that $\iota_1 \cup \cdots \cup \iota_m$ is a partial function as required.

For the lexicon of the running example, the base is:

{ {lang=German, lemma=fahren, pos=V,
gloss=drive,
example=Ein Fahrrad fahren},
{lang=German, lemma=fahren, pos=V,
gloss=go,
example=Er ist mit dem Zug gefahren},
{lang=German, lemma=Fahrrad, pos=N,
gloss=bicycle,
example=Ein Fahrrad fahren},
{lang=German, lemma=Fahrrad, pos=N,
gloss=bicycle,
example=Mein Fahrrad hat einen Platten} }.

There are many different lexica however that share the same base. This is illustrated by Figure 3. We see that the information is presented in an entirely different fashion, with a focus on the examples.

In a lexicon such as that in Figure 2, there may be nodes labelled 'Meaning' without any children corresponding to attribute 'example'. This means that there would be items ι in $B(L)$ such that $\iota(\text{example})$ is undefined. For some of the constructions and proofs below, it is convenient to circumvent this complication, by assuming special 'null' values for absent leaf nodes for attributes. As a result, we may treat an item as a complete function rather than as a partial function on the domain A.

There is a certain resemblance between the base of a lexicon and the disjunctive normal form of a logical expression, the attribute-value pairs taking the place of propositional variables, and the items

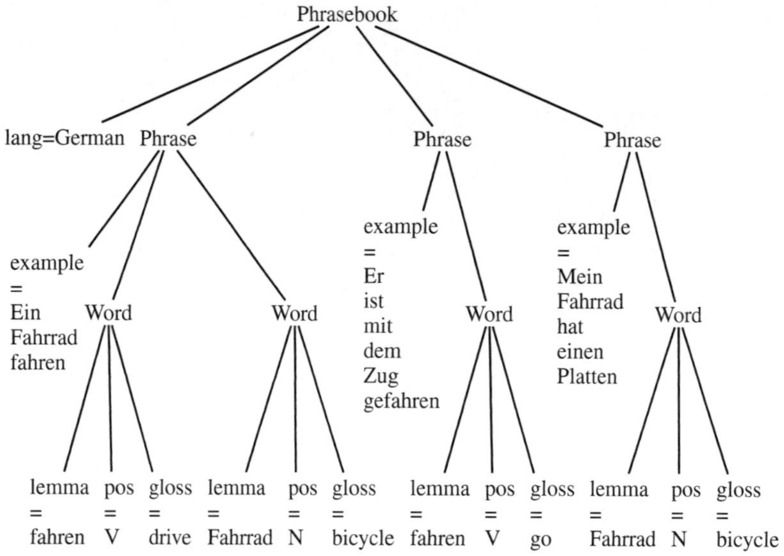

Figure 3: A lexicon L' with the same base as the one in Figure 2.

taking the place of conjunctions. Thus our semantic interpretation of lexica is such that two siblings in the tree are regarded as alternatives (disjunction) if their labels contain the same attribute or component, and they are regarded as joint information (conjunction) if their labels contain distinct attributes or components.

Theorem 1 *For each lexicon base $B = (A_B, V, I)$ and for each lexicon schema $S = (A_S, C, T)$ with $A_B \subseteq A_S$, there is a lexicon L that is an instance of S and whose base is B.*

Proof Assume the root r of T has only one child r'. (Otherwise, make S extended first.) Let T' be the subtree of T at r'. For each item $\iota \in I$, create a copy of T', denoted by t_ι. At each leaf node of t_ι, supplement the label a with the corresponding value from ι if any; if a does not occur in ι, then remove the leaf node from t_ι. (If the parent of a removed leaf node has no other children, then also remove the parent, etc.) Create a root node, with the same label as r, the children of which are the roots of the respective t_ι. Let the resulting tree be called t. The requirements of the theorem are now satisfied by $L = (A_B, V, C, t)$. ∎

3 Lexicon transformations

As we have seen, the information contained in one lexicon base may be rendered in different structural forms, in terms of lexica. The structure of a lexicon is isolated from its content by means of a lexicon schema. In this section we will address the question how we may formalize transformations from one lexicon schema S_1 to lexicon schema S_2, or more precisely, from one class of lexica that are instances of S_1 to another class of lexica that are instances of S_2. In fact, for the sake of the definitions below, we assume that the input to a transformation is not a lexicon but its base, which contains all the necessary information. (That the actual implementation mentioned in Section 1 may often avoid expansion to the base need not concern us here.)

A *lexicon transformation* R is a tuple (A, C, τ), where A is a finite set of attributes as before, C is a finite set of components as before, and τ is a labelled, unordered tree such that:

- each leaf node is labelled by an element from A,
- the root node is labelled by an element from C,
- each internal node is either labelled by an element from C, or by a subset of A,
- each element from $A \cup C$ occurs exactly once as a label by itself,
- each element from A occurs exactly once in a label that is a subset of A, and
- each node ν labelled by a set $\{a_1, \ldots, a_k\} \subseteq A$ has exactly one child, which is labelled

by an element from $A \cup C$, and the leaves labelled $a_1, \ldots, a_k$ are each descendants of ν.

A lexicon transformation is very similar to a lexicon schema, except for the extra nodes labelled by sets $A' \subseteq A$ of attributes, which we refer to as *restrictors*. Such a node indicates that for the purpose of the subtree, one should commit to particular subsets of the input lexicon base. Each such subset is determined by a choice of a fixed value for each attribute in A'.

As an example, consider the lexicon transformations in Figure 4(a) and (b). If we omit the nodes labelled by restrictors, then we obtain a lexicon schema. In the case of (b), this is the lexicon schema in Figure 1. In Figure 4(a), the node labelled $\{\text{example}\}$ means that the transformation takes one non-empty subset of the base for each possible value of attribute 'example'. For each subset, one node labelled 'Phrase' is generated in the target lexicon. At the node labelled $\{\text{lemma}, \text{pos}\}$, the subset of the base is further restricted, and for each combination of a value of 'lemma' and a value of 'pos' in the current subset of items, a node labelled 'Word' is generated. If the base contains several glosses for one choice of 'example', 'lemma' and 'pos', each such gloss leads to a separate leaf node.

The meaning of a lexicon transformation is formally expressed in Figure 5. A call $lexicon(\nu, I')$, where ν is a node of τ and I' is a subset of I from the input lexicon base $B = (A, V, I)$, returns a set of nodes. The function is recursive, in that the value of $lexicon(\nu, I')$ is expressed in terms of values of $lexicon(\nu', I'')$ for child nodes ν' of ν and subsets I'' of I'. The main purpose is the computation of $lexicon(\rho, I)$, where ρ is the root of τ. As ρ is labelled by an element from C, $lexicon(\rho, I)$ is by definition a singleton set $\{r\}$, with r becoming the root of the resulting lexicon.

Note that the placement of restrictors is critical. For example, if we were to move up the restrictor $\{\text{gloss}\}$ in Figure 4(b) to merge with the restrictor $\{\text{lemma}, \text{pos}\}$, this would result in one entry for each combination of 'lemma', 'pos' and 'gloss', and in each entry there would be at most one meaning. It is not apparent that such a choice would be less appropriate than the choice we made in Figures 2 and 4(b). However, if we were to move down the node labelled $\{\text{gloss}\}$ to become a child of the node labelled 'Meaning' and a parent

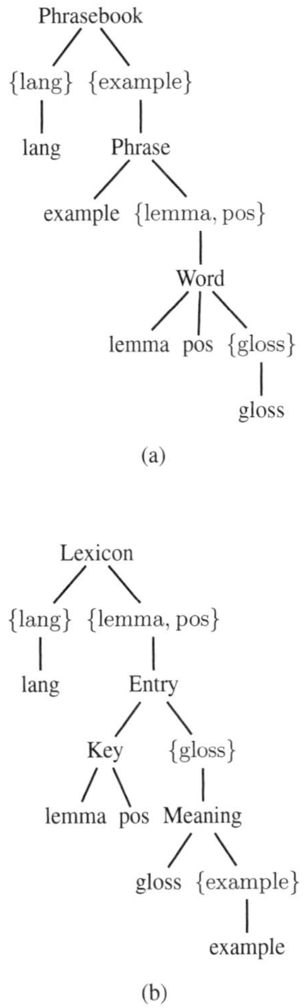

Figure 4: Two lexicon transformations: (a) is capable of mapping the base of lexicon L (Figure 2) to lexicon L' (Figure 3), and (b) is capable of the reverse mapping.

of the leaf node labelled 'gloss', then we would lose the coupling between glosses and examples, which seems undesirable. This observation underlies much of the development in Section 5.

4 Completeness

Next, we investigate whether the lexicon transformations as we defined them are powerful enough to produce 'reasonable' lexica starting from a lexicon base. As unreasonable, we reject those lexica that contain information that cannot be expressed in terms of a base. This concerns siblings in the tree with the same component label. How many siblings with the same component should be generated can be deduced from the base, provided we may assume that there is a combination of attribute values that distinguishes one sibling from another.

$lexicon(\nu, I')$:
  if the label of ν is $a \in A$
    let v be the (only) value such that $\exists \iota \in I'[\iota(a) = v]$
    create a new node n with label (a, v)
    return $\{n\}$
  else if the label of ν is $c \in C$
    let the children of ν be $\nu_1, \ldots, \nu_m$
    create a new node n with label c and children $\bigcup_{1 \leq i \leq m} lexicon(\nu_i, I')$
    return $\{n\}$
  else if the label of ν is $A' = \{a_1, \ldots, a_k\} \subseteq A$
    let the only child of ν be ν'
    let **I** be the set of all I'' such that there is a combination of
      $v_1, \ldots, v_k \in V$ with $I'' = \{\iota \in I' \mid \iota(a_1) = v_1, \ldots, \iota(a_k) = v_k\} \neq \emptyset$
    return $\bigcup_{I'' \in \mathbf{I}} lexicon(\nu', I'')$

Figure 5: The meaning of a lexicon transformation, as a recursive function. The return value is a set of nodes that are created. The main application is $lexicon(\rho, I)$, where ρ is the root of τ and I is taken from the input lexicon base.

We call such a combination of attributes a *key*.

Formally, a *key mapping* for a lexicon schema (A, C, T) is a function f that maps each component from C to a subset of A, subject to the following restrictions. Let c be a component and let n be the node of T that is labelled by c. Then for each attribute a in key $f(c)$, the leaf node of T that is labelled by a should be a descendant of n. The component that occurs as label of the root of T is always mapped to the empty set of attributes, and may be ignored in the following discussion.

Let lexicon $L = (A_L, V, C_L, t)$ be an instance of schema $S = (A_S, C_S, T)$. We say that L *satisfies* the key mapping f for S if:

1. among the leaves, there is no pair of distinct siblings in t with identical labels, and

2. for each maximal set $\{n_1, \ldots, n_m\}$ of siblings in t labelled by the same component c, with $f(c) = \{a_1, \ldots, a_k\}$, we have that for each i ($1 \leq i \leq m$), there is a distinct combination of values $v_1, \ldots, v_k \in V$ such that:

$$I(n_i) = \{\iota \in \bigcup_{1 \leq j \leq m} I(n_j) \mid \iota(a_1) = v_1, \ldots, \iota(a_k) = v_k\}.$$

The second condition states that the total set of items coming from all siblings with the same label c is partitioned on the basis of distinct combinations of values for attributes from the key, and the subsets of the partition come from the respective siblings.

Returning to the running example, the lexicon L in Figure 2 satisfies the key mapping f given by:

$$\begin{array}{lcl} f(\text{Lexicon}) & = & \emptyset \\ f(\text{Entry}) & = & \{\text{lemma}, \text{pos}\} \\ f(\text{Key}) & = & \emptyset \\ f(\text{Meaning}) & = & \{\text{gloss}\} \end{array}$$

A different key mapping exists for the lexicon L' in Figure 3.

If n_1 and n_2 are two distinct nodes in the tree T of schema S, with labels c_1 and c_2, respectively, then we may assume that $f(c_1)$ and $f(c_2)$ are disjoint, for the following reason. Suppose that the intersection of $f(c_1)$ and $f(c_2)$ includes an attribute a, then n_1 must be a descendant of n_2 or vice versa, because the leaf labelled a must be a descendant of both n_1 and n_2. Assume that n_1 is a descendant of n_2. As the base is already restricted at n_1 to items ι with $\iota(a) = v$, for certain v, a may be omitted from $f(c_2)$ without changing the semantics of the key mapping. This observation is used in the construction in the proof of the following.

Theorem 2 *Let lexicon $L = (A_L, V, C_L, t)$ be an instance of schema $S = (A_S, C_S, T)$, satisfying key mapping f. Then there is a lexicon transformation that maps $B(L)$ to L.*

Proof The required lexicon transformation is constructed out of T and f. We insert an additional restrictor node just above each non-leaf node labelled c, and as the restrictor we take $f(c)$.

(If $f(c) = \emptyset$, we may abstain from adding a restrictor node.) If an attribute a does not occur in $f(c)$, for any $c \in C_S$, then we add a restrictor node with set $\{a\}$ just above the leaf node labelled a. The result is the tree τ of a lexicon transformation $R = (A_S, C_S, \tau)$.

It is now straightforward to prove that R maps $B(L)$ to L, by induction on the height of T, on the basis of the close similarity between the structure of T and the structure of τ, and the close link between the chosen restrictors and the keys from which they were constructed. ∎

For the running example, the construction in the proof above leads to the transformation in Figure 4(b).

Theorem 2 reveals the conditions under which the structure of a lexicon can be retrieved from its base, by means of a transformation. Simultaneously, it shows the completeness of the type of lexicon transformation that we proposed. If a lexicon L is given, and if an alternative lexicon L' with $B(L') = B(L)$ exists that is an instance of some schema S and that is 'reasonable' in the sense that it satisfies a key mapping for S, then L' can be effectively constructed from L by the derived transformation.

5 Consistency

We now investigate the conditions under which a lexicon transformation preserves the base. The starting point is the observation at the end of Section 3, where we argued that if a restrictor is chosen too low in the tree τ relative to other restrictors, then some necessary dependence between attribute values is lost. Note that the proof of Theorem 1 suggests that having only one restrictor with all attributes at the root of the tree always preserves the base, but the result would be unsatisfactory in practice.

For a set A of attributes, we define an *independence system* D as a set of triples (A_1, A_2, A_3) where A_1, A_2, $A_3 \subseteq A$ and $A_1 \cap A_2 = \emptyset$. We pronounce $(A_1, A_2, A_3) \in D$ as 'A_1 and A_2 are independent under A_3'. It should be noted that A_3 may overlap with A_1 and with A_2.

We say a lexicon base (A, V, I) *satisfies* D if for each $(A_1, A_2, A_3) \in D$ with $A_1 = \{a_{1,1}, \ldots a_{1,k_1}\}$, $A_2 = \{a_{2,1}, \ldots a_{2,k_2}\}$, $A_3 = \{a_{3,1}, \ldots a_{3,k_3}\}$, and for each combination of values $v_{1,1}, \ldots, v_{1,k_1}, v_{2,1}, \ldots, v_{2,k_2}, v_{3,1}, \ldots, v_{3,k_3}$, we have:

$$\begin{aligned}
&\exists \iota \in I[\iota(a_{1,1}) = v_{1,1} \wedge \ldots \wedge \iota(a_{1,k_1}) = v_{1,k_1} \wedge \\
&\qquad \iota(a_{3,1}) = v_{3,1} \wedge \ldots \wedge \iota(a_{3,k_3}) = v_{3,k_3}] \wedge \\
&\exists \iota \in I[\iota(a_{2,1}) = v_{2,1} \wedge \ldots \wedge \iota(a_{2,k_2}) = v_{2,k_2} \wedge \\
&\qquad \iota(a_{3,1}) = v_{3,1} \wedge \ldots \wedge \iota(a_{3,k_3}) = v_{3,k_3}] \\
&\Longrightarrow \\
&\exists \iota \in I[\iota(a_{1,1}) = v_{1,1} \wedge \ldots \wedge \iota(a_{1,k_1}) = v_{1,k_1} \wedge \\
&\qquad \iota(a_{2,1}) = v_{2,1} \wedge \ldots \wedge \iota(a_{2,k_2}) = v_{2,k_2} \wedge \\
&\qquad \iota(a_{3,1}) = v_{3,1} \wedge \ldots \wedge \iota(a_{3,k_3}) = v_{3,k_3}].
\end{aligned}$$

The intuition is that as long as the values for A_3 are fixed, allowable combinations of values for $A_1 \cup A_2$ in I can be found by looking at A_1 and A_2 individually.

We say that a lexicon transformation $R = (A, C, \tau)$ is *allowed* by an independence system D if the following condition is satisfied for each node ν in τ that is labelled by a component c and a node ν' that is its child: Let A_1 be the set of attributes at leaves that are descendants of ν', and let A_2 be the set of attributes at leaves that are descendants of the other children of ν. Let A_3 be the union of the restrictors at ancestors of ν. Now (A_1, A_2, A_3) should be in D.

Theorem 3 *If a lexicon base $B = (A, V, I)$ satisfies an independence system D, if a lexicon transformation R is allowed by D, and if R maps B to lexicon L, then $B(L) = B$.*

The proof by induction on the height of τ is fairly straightforward but tedious.

In the running example, there are a number of triples in D but most are trivial, such as $(\emptyset, \{\text{gloss}, \text{example}\}, \{\text{lemma}, \text{pos}\})$. Another triple in D is $(\{\text{lang}\}, \{\text{lemma}, \text{pos}, \text{gloss}, \text{example}\}, \emptyset)$, but only because we assume in this example that one lexicon is designed for one language only. In general, there will be more interesting independency, typically if a lexical entry consists of a number of unconnected units, for example one explaining syntactic usage of a word, another explaining semantic usage, and another presenting information on etymology.

The implication of Theorem 3 is that transformations between lexica preserve the information that they represent, as long as the transformations respect the dependencies between sets of attributes. Within these bounds, an attribute a may be located in a restrictor in τ anywhere between the root node and the leaf node labelled a.

6 Implementation

The mathematical framework in this paper models a restricted case of merging and restructuring a number of input lexica. An implementation was developed as a potential new module of LEXUS, which is a web-based tool for manipulating lexical resources, as described by Kemps-Snijders et al. (2006).

The restriction considered here involves only one input lexicon, and we have abstracted away from a large number of features present in the actual implementation, among which are provisions to interact with the user, to access external linguistic functions (e.g. morphological operations), and to rename attributes. These simplifications have allowed us to isolate one essential and difficult problem of lexicon merging, namely how to carry over the underlying information from one lexicon to another, in spite of possible significant differences in structure.

The framework considered here assumes that during construction of the target lexicon, the information present in the source lexicon is repeatedly narrowed down by restrictors, as explained in Section 3. Each restrictor amounts to a loop over all combinations of the relevant attribute values from the currently considered part of the source lexicon.

Let us consider a path from the root of the lexicon transformation to a leaf, which may comprise several restrictors. The number of combinations of attribute values considered is bounded by an exponential function on the total number of attributes contained in those restrictors. Motivated by this consideration, we have chosen to regard a lexicon transformation as if its input were an expanded form of the source lexicon, or in other words, a lexicon base.

However, in terms of the actual implementation, the discussed form of restrictors must be seen as a worst case, which is able to realize some of the most invasive types of restructuring. Next to restrictors that select combinations of attribute values, our lexicon transformations also allow primitives that each represent a loop over all *nodes* of the presently considered part of the source lexicon that are labelled by a chosen component or attribute. By using only such primitives, the time complexity remains polynomial in the size of the input lexicon and the size of the input lexicon transformation. This requires an implementation that does not expand the information contained in a source lexicon in terms of a lexicon base. A full description of the implementation would go beyond the context of this paper.

7 Conclusions

We have introduced a class of lexicon transformations, and have shown interesting completeness and consistency properties.

The restrictors in our lexicon transformations are able to repeatedly narrow down the information contained in the source lexicon based on attribute values, while constructing the target lexicon from the top down. Existing types of tree manipulations, such as tree transducers, do not possess the ability to repeatedly narrow down a *set* of considered nodes scattered throughout a source structure, and therefore seem to be incapable of expressing types of lexicon transformations allowing the completeness results we have seen in this paper.

One could in principle implement our lexicon transformations in terms of technologies such as XQuery and XSLT, but only in the sense that these formalisms are Turing complete. Our restrictors do not have a direct equivalent in these formalisms, which would make our type of lexicon transformation cumbersome to express in XQuery or XSLT. At the same time, their Turing completeness makes XQuery and XSLT too powerful to be of practical use for the specification of lexicon transformations.

A tentative conclusion seems to be that our class of lexicon transformations has useful properties not shared by a number of existing theories involving tree manipulations. This justifies further study.

Acknowledgements

This work was done while the author was employed at the Max Planck Institute for Psycholinguistics. The work was motivated by suggestions from Peter Wittenburg and Marc Kemps-Snijders, whose input is gratefully acknowledged.

References

D. Chan Ka-Leung and D. Wu. 1999. Automatically merging lexicons that have incompatible part-of-speech categories. In *Joint SIGDAT Conference on Empirical Methods in Natural Language Processing and Very Large Corpora*, pages 247–257, University of Maryland, USA, June.

G. Francopoulo, N. Bel, M. George, N. Calzolari, M. Monachini, M. Pet, and C. Soria. 2006. Lexical markup framework (LMF) for NLP multilingual resources. In *Proceedings of the Workshop on Multilingual Language Resources and Interoperability*, pages 1–8, Sydney, Australia, July.

Z. Fülöp and H. Vogler. 1998. *Syntax-Directed Semantics: Formal Models Based on Tree Transducers*. Springer, Berlin.

E.R. Harold and W.S. Means. 2004. *XML in a Nutshell*. O'Reilly.

H. Jing, Y. Dahan Netzer, M. Elhadad, and K.R. McKeown. 2000. Integrating a large-scale, reusable lexicon with a natural language generator. In *Proceedings of the First International Conference on Natural Language Generation*, pages 209–216, Mitzpe Ramon, Israel, June.

M. Kemps-Snijders, M.-J. Nederhof, and P. Wittenburg. 2006. LEXUS, a web-based tool for manipulating lexical resources. In *LREC 2006: Fifth International Conference on Language Resources and Evaluation, Proceedings*, pages 1862–1865.

J.W. Lloyd. 1984. *Foundations of Logic Programming*. Springer-Verlag.

M. Monachini, F. Calzolari, M. Mammini, S. Rossi, and M. Ulivieri. 2004. Unifying lexicons in view of a phonological and morphological lexical DB. In *LREC 2004: Fourth International Conference on Language Resources and Evaluation*, pages 1107–1110, Lisbon, Portugal, May.

N. Ruimy. 2006. Merging two ontology-based lexical resources. In *LREC 2006: Fifth International Conference on Language Resources and Evaluation, Proceedings*, pages 1716–1721.

P. Walmsley. 2007. *XQuery*. O'Reilly.

n-Best Parsing Revisited*

Matthias Büchse and **Daniel Geisler** and **Torsten Stüber** and **Heiko Vogler**
Faculty of Computer Science
Technische Universität Dresden
01062 Dresden
{buechse,geisler,stueber,vogler}@tcs.inf.tu-dresden.de

Abstract

We derive and implement an algorithm similar to (Huang and Chiang, 2005) for finding the n best derivations in a weighted hypergraph. We prove the correctness and termination of the algorithm and we show experimental results concerning its runtime. Our work is different from the aforementioned one in the following respects: we consider labeled hypergraphs, allowing for tree-based language models (Maletti and Satta, 2009); we specifically handle the case of cyclic hypergraphs; we admit structured weight domains, allowing for multiple features to be processed; we use the paradigm of functional programming together with lazy evaluation, achieving concise algorithmic descriptions.

1 Introduction

In statistical natural language processing, probabilistic models play an important role which can be used to assign to some input sentence a set of analyses, each carrying a probability. For instance, an analysis can be a parse tree or a possible translation. Due to the ambiguity of natural language, the number of analyses for one input sentence can be very large. Some models even assign an infinite number of analyses to an input sentence.

In many cases however, the set of analyses can in fact be represented in a finite and compact way. While such a representation is space-efficient, it may be incompatible with subsequent operations. In these cases a finite subset is used as an approximation, consisting of n best analyses, i. e. n analyses with highest probability. For example, this approach has the following two applications.

(1) Reranking: when log-linear models (Och and Ney, 2002) are employed, some features may not permit an efficient evaluation during the computation of the analyses. These features are computed using individual analyses from said approximation, leading to a reranking amongst them.

(2) Spurious ambiguity: many models produce analyses which may be too fine-grained for further processing (Li et al., 2009). As an example, consider context-free grammars, where several leftmost derivations may exist for the same terminal string. The weight of the terminal string is obtained by summing over these derivations. The n best leftmost derivations may be used to approximate this sum.

In this paper, we consider the case where the finite, compact representation has the form of a weighted hypergraph (with labeled hyperedges) and the analyses are derivations of the hypergraph. This covers many parsing applications (Klein and Manning, 2001), including weighted deductive systems (Goodman, 1999; Nederhof, 2003), and also applications in machine translation (May and Knight, 2006).

In the nomenclature of (Huang and Chiang, 2005), which we adopt here, a derivation of a hypergraph is a tree which is obtained in the following way. Starting from some node, an ingoing hyperedge is picked and recorded as the label of the root of the tree. Then, for the subtrees, one continues with the source nodes of said hyperedge in the same way. In other words, a derivation can be understood as an unfolding of the hypergraph.

The n-best-derivations problem then amounts to finding n derivations which are best with respect to the weights induced by the weighted hypergraph.[1] Among others, weighted hypergraphs with labeled hyperedges subsume the following two concepts.

(I) probabilistic context-free grammars (pcfgs).

* This research was financially supported by DFG VO 1101/5-1.

[1] Note that this problem is different from the n-best-hyperpaths problem described by Nielsen et al. (2005), as already argued in (Huang and Chiang, 2005, Section 2).

Proceedings of the 2010 Workshop on Applications of Tree Automata in Natural Language Processing, ACL 2010, pages 46–54, Uppsala, Sweden, 16 July 2010.

In this case, nodes correspond to nonterminals, hyperedges are labeled with productions, and the derivations are exactly the abstract syntax trees (ASTs) of the grammar (which are closely related the parse trees). Note that, unless the pcfg is unambiguous, a given word may have several corresponding ASTs, and its weight is obtained by summing over the weights of the ASTs. Hence, the n best derivations need not coincide with the n best words (cf. application (2) above).

(II) weighted tree automata (wta) (Alexandrakis and Bozapalidis, 1987; Berstel and Reutenauer, 1982; Ésik and Kuich, 2003; Fülöp and Vogler, 2009). These automata serve both as a tree-based language model and as a data structure for the parse forests obtained from that language model by applying the Bar-Hillel construction (Maletti and Satta, 2009). It is well known that context-free grammars and tree automata are weakly equivalent (Thatcher, 1967; Ésik and Kuich, 2003). However, unlike the former formalism, the latter one has the ability to model non-local dependencies in parse trees.

In the case of wta, nodes correspond to states, hyperedges are labeled with input symbols, and the derivations are exactly the runs of the automaton. Since, due to ambiguity, a given tree may have several accepting runs, the n best derivations need not coincide with the n best trees. As for the pcfgs, this is an example of spurious ambiguity, which can be tackled as indicated by application (2) above. Alternatively, one can attempt to find an equivalent deterministic wta (May and Knight, 2006; Büchse et al., 2009).

Next, we briefly discuss four known algorithms which solve the n-best-derivations problem or subproblems thereof.

• The Viterbi algorithm solves the 1-best-derivation problem for acyclic hypergraphs. It is based on a topological sort of the hypergraph.

• Knuth (1977) generalizes Dijkstra's algorithm (for finding the single-source shortest paths in a graph) to hypergraphs, thus solving the case $n = 1$ even if the hypergraph contains cycles. Knuth assumes the weights to be real numbers, and he requires weight functions to be monotone and superior in order to guarantee that a best derivation exists. (The superiority property corresponds to Dijkstra's requirement that edge weights—or, more generally, cycle weights—are nonnegative.)

• Huang and Chiang (2005) show that the n-best-derivations problem can be solved efficiently by first solving the 1-best-derivation problem and then extending that solution in a lazy manner. Huang and Chiang assume weighted unlabeled hypergraphs with weights computed in the reals, and they require the weight functions to be monotone.

Moreover they assume that the 1-best-derivation problem be solved using the Viterbi algorithm, which implies that the hypergraph must be acyclic. However they conjecture that their second phase also works for cyclic hypergraphs.

• Pauls and Klein (2009) propose a variation of the algorithm of Huang and Chiang (2005) in which the 1-best-derivation problem is computed via an A^*-based exploration of the 1-best charts.

In this paper, we also present an algorithm for solving the n-best-derivations problem. Ultimately it uses the same algorithmic ideas as the one of Huang and Chiang (2005); however, it is different in the following sense:

1. we consider labeled hypergraphs, allowing for wta to be used in parsing;
2. we specifically handle the case of cyclic hypergraphs, thus supporting the conjecture of Huang and Chiang; for this we impose on the weight functions the same requirements as Knuth and use his algorithm;
3. by using the concept of linear pre-orders (and not only linear orders on the set of reals) our approach can handle structured weights such as vectors over frequencies, probabilities, and reals;
4. we present our algorithm in the framework of functional programming (and not in that of imperative programming); this framework allows to decribe algorithms in a more abstract and concise, yet natural way;
5. due to the lazy evaluation paradigm often found in functional programming, we obtain the laziness on which the algorithm of Huang and Chiang (2005) is based for free;
6. exploiting the abstract level of description (see point 4) we are able to prove the correctness and termination of our algorithm.

At the end of this paper, we will discuss experiments which have been performed with an implementation of our algorithm in the functional programming language HASKELL.

2 The n-best-derivations problem

In this section, we state the n-best-derivations problem formally, and we give a comprehensive example. First, we introduce some basic notions.

Trees and hypergraphs The definition of ranked trees commonly used in formal tree language theory will serve us as the basis for defining derivations.

A *ranked alphabet* is a finite set Σ (of *symbols*) where every symbol carries a *rank* (a nonnegative integer). By $\Sigma^{(k)}$ we denote the set of those symbols having rank k. The *set of trees over* Σ, denoted by T_Σ, is the smallest set T such that for every $k \in \mathbb{N}$, $\sigma \in \Sigma^{(k)}$, and $\xi_1, \ldots, \xi_k \in T$, also $\sigma(\xi_1, \ldots, \xi_k) \in T$;[2] for $\sigma \in \Sigma^{(0)}$ we abbreviate $\sigma()$ by σ. For every $k \in \mathbb{N}$, $\sigma \in \Sigma^{(k)}$ and subsets $T_1, \ldots, T_k \subseteq T_\Sigma$ we define the *top-concatenation (with σ)* $\sigma(T_1, \ldots, T_k) = \{\sigma(\xi_1, \ldots, \xi_k) \mid \xi_1 \in T_1, \ldots, \xi_k \in T_k\}$.

A Σ-*hypergraph* is a pair $H = (V, E)$ where V is a finite set (of *vertices* or *nodes*) and $E \subseteq V^* \times \Sigma \times V$ is a finite set (of *hyperedges*) such that for every $(v_1 \ldots v_k, \sigma, v) \in E$ we have that $\sigma \in \Sigma^{(k)}$.[3] We interpret E as a ranked alphabet where the rank of each edge is carried over from its label in Σ. The family $(H_v \mid v \in V)$ of *derivations of* H is the smallest family $(P_v \mid v \in V)$ of subsets of T_E such that $e(P_{v_1}, \ldots, P_{v_k}) \subseteq P_v$ for every $e = (v_1 \ldots v_k, \sigma, v) \in E$.

A Σ-hypergraph (V, E) is *cyclic* if there are hyperedges $(v_1^1 \ldots v_{k_1}^1, \sigma_1, v^1)$, $\ldots$, $(v_1^l \ldots v_{k_l}^l, \sigma_l, v^l) \in E$ such that v^{j-1} occurs in $v_1^j \ldots v_{k_j}^j$ for every $j \in \{2, \ldots, l\}$ and v^l occurs in $v_1^1 \ldots v_{k_1}^1$. It is called *acyclic* if it is not cyclic.

Example 1 Consider the ranked alphabet $\Sigma = \Sigma^{(0)} \cup \Sigma^{(1)} \cup \Sigma^{(2)}$ with $\Sigma^{(0)} = \{\alpha, \beta\}$, $\Sigma^{(1)} = \{\gamma\}$, and $\Sigma^{(2)} = \{\sigma\}$, and the Σ-hypergraph $H = (V, E)$ where

- $V = \{0, 1\}$ and
- $E = \{(\varepsilon, \alpha, 1), (\varepsilon, \beta, 1), (1, \gamma, 1), (11, \sigma, 0), (1, \gamma, 0)\}$.

A graphical representation of this hypergraph is shown in Fig. 1. Note that this hypergraph is cyclic because of the edge $(1, \gamma, 1)$.

We indicate the derivations of H, assuming that $e_1, \ldots, e_5$ are the edges in E in the order given above:

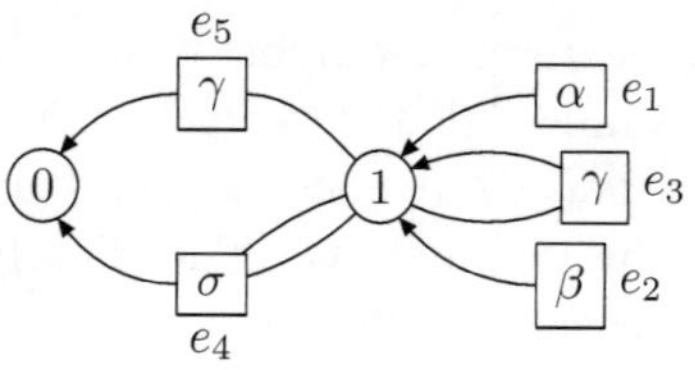

Figure 1: Hypergraph of Example 1.

- $H_1 = \{e_1, e_2, e_3(e_1), e_3(e_2), e_3(e_3(e_1)), \ldots\}$ and
- $H_0 = e_4(H_1, H_1) \cup e_5(H_1)$ where, e. g., $e_4(H_1, H_1)$ is the top-concatenation of H_1, H_1 with e_4, and thus

$$e_4(H_1,H_1) = \{e_4(e_1, e_1), e_4(e_1, e_2), e_4(e_1, e_3(e_1)), e_4(e_3(e_1), e_1), \ldots\}.$$

Next we give an example of ambiguity in hypergraphs with labeled hyperedges. Suppose that E contains an additional hyperedge $e_6 = (0, \gamma, 0)$. Then H_0 would contain the derivations $e_6(e_5(e_1))$ and $e_5(e_3(e_1))$, which describe the same Σ-tree, viz. $\gamma(\gamma(\alpha))$ (obtained by the node-wise projection to the second component). □

In the sequel, let $H = (V, E)$ be a Σ-hypergraph.

Ordering Usually an ordering is induced on the set of derivations by means of probabilities or, more generally, weights. In the following, we will abstract from the weights by using a binary relation $\precsim$ *directly* on derivations, where we will interpret the fact $\xi_1 \precsim \xi_2$ as "ξ_1 is better than or equal to ξ_2".

Example 2 (Ex. 1 contd.) First we show how an ordering is induced on derivations by means of weights. To this end, we associate an operation over the set $\mathbb{R}$ of reals with every hyperedge (respecting its arity) by means of a mapping θ:

$$\theta(e_1)() = 4 \qquad \theta(e_2)() = 3$$
$$\theta(e_3)(x_1) = x_1 + 1 \qquad \theta(e_4)(x_1, x_2) = x_1 + x_2$$
$$\theta(e_5)(x_1) = x_1 + 0.5$$

The weight $h(\xi)$ of a tree $\xi \in T_E$ is obtained by interpreting the symbols at each node using θ, e. g. $h(e_3(e_2)) = \theta(e_3)(\theta(e_2)()) = \theta(e_2)() + 1 = 4$.

Then the natural order $\leq$ on $\mathbb{R}$ induces the binary relation $\precsim$ over T_E as follows: for every $\xi_1, \xi_2 \in T_E$ we let $\xi_1 \precsim \xi_2$ iff $h(\xi_1) \leq h(\xi_2)$, meaning that trees with smaller weights are considered better. (This is, e. g., the case when calculating probabilites in the image of $-\log x$.) Note

[2] The term $\sigma(\xi_1, \ldots, \xi_k)$ is usually understood as a string composed of the symbol σ, an opening parenthesis, the string ξ_1, a comma, and so on.

[3] The hypergraphs defined here are essentially nondeterministic tree automata, where V is the set of states and E is the set of transitions.

that we could just as well have defined $\precsim$ with the inverted order.

Since addition is commutative, we obtain for every $\xi_1, \xi_2 \in T_E$ that $h(e_4(\xi_1, \xi_2)) = h(e_4(\xi_2, \xi_1))$ and thus $e_4(\xi_1, \xi_2) \precsim e_4(\xi_2, \xi_1)$ and vice versa. Thus, for two different trees ($e_4(\xi_1, \xi_2)$ and $e_4(\xi_2, \xi_1)$) having the same weight, $\precsim$ should not prefer any of them. That is, $\precsim$ need not be antisymmetric.

As another example, the mapping θ could assign to each symbol an operation over real-valued vectors, where each component represents one feature of a log-linear model such as frequencies, probabilities, reals, etc. Then the ordering could be defined by means of a linear combination of the feature weights. □

We use the concept of a linear pre-order to capture the orderings which are obtained this way.

Let S be a set. A *pre-order (on S)* is a binary relation $\precsim \subseteq S \times S$ such that (i) $s \precsim s$ for every $s \in S$ (*reflexivity*) and (ii) $s_1 \precsim s_2$ and $s_2 \precsim s_3$ implies $s_1 \precsim s_3$ for every $s_1, s_2, s_3 \in S$ (*transitivity*). A pre-order $\precsim$ is called *linear* if $s_1 \precsim s_2$ or $s_2 \precsim s_1$ for every $s_1, s_2 \in S$. For instance, the binary relation $\precsim$ on T_E as defined in Ex. 2 is a linear pre-order.

We will restrict our considerations to a class of linear pre-orders which admit efficient algorithms. For this, we will always assume a linear pre-order $\precsim$ with the following two properties (cf. Knuth (1977)).[4]

SP (*subtree property*) For every $e(\xi_1, \ldots, \xi_k) \in T_E$ and $i \in \{1, \ldots, k\}$ we have $\xi_i \precsim e(\xi_1, \ldots, \xi_k)$.[5]

CP (*compatibility*) For every pair $e(\xi_1, \ldots, \xi_k)$, $e(\xi'_1, \ldots, \xi'_k) \in T_E$ with $\xi_1 \precsim \xi'_1$, …, $\xi_k \precsim \xi'_k$ we have that $e(\xi_1, \ldots, \xi_k) \precsim e(\xi'_1, \ldots, \xi'_k)$.

It is easy to verify that the linear pre-order $\precsim$ of Ex. 2 has the aforementioned properties.

> *In the sequel, let $\precsim$ be a linear pre-order on T_E fulfilling SP and CP.*

[4]Originally, these properties were called "superiority" and "monotonicity" because they were viewed as properties of the weight functions. We use the terms "subtree property" and "compatibility" respectively, because we view them as properties of the linear pre-order.

[5]This strong property is used here for simplicity. It suffices to require that for every $v \in V$ and pair $\xi, \xi' \in H_v$ we have $\xi \precsim \xi'$ if ξ is a subtree of ξ'.

Before we state the n-best-derivations problem formally, we define the operation $\min_n$, which maps every subset T of T_E to the set of all sequences of n best elements of T. To this end, let $T \subseteq T_E$ and $n \leq |T|$. We define $\min_n(T)$ to be the set of all sequences $(\xi_1, \ldots, \xi_n) \in T^n$ of pairwise distinct elements such that $\xi_1 \precsim \ldots \precsim \xi_n$ and for every $\xi \in T \setminus \{\xi_1, \ldots, \xi_k\}$ we have $\xi_n \precsim \xi$. For every $n > |T|$ we set $\min_n(T) = \min_{|T|}(T)$. In addition, we set $\min_{\leq n}(T) = \bigcup_{i=0}^{n} \min_i(T)$.

n-best-derivations problem The *n-best-derivations problem* amounts to the following.

Given a Σ-hypergraph $H = (V, E)$, a vertex $v \in V$, and a linear pre-order $\precsim$ on T_E fulfilling SP and CP,

compute an element of $\min_n(H_v)$.

3 Functional Programming

We will describe our main algorithm as a functional program. In essence, such a program is a system of (recursive) equations that defines several functions (as shown in Fig. 2). As a consequence the main computational paradigm for evaluating the application `(f a)` of a function `f` to an argument `a` is to choose an appropriate defining equation `f x = r` and then evaluate `(f a)` to `r'` which is obtained from `r` by substituting every occurrence of `x` by `a`.

We assume a *lazy* (and in particular, *call-by-need*) evaluation strategy, as in the functional programming language HASKELL. Roughly speaking, this amounts to evaluating the arguments of a function only as needed to evaluate the its body (i. e. for branching). If an argument occurs multiple times in the body, it is evaluated only once.

We use HASKELL notation and functions for dealing with lists, i. e. we denote the empty list by `[]` and list construction by `x:xs` (where an element `x` is prepended to a list `xs`), and we use the functions `head` (line 01), `tail` (line 02), and `take` (lines 03 and 04), which return the first element in a list, a list without its first element, and a prefix of a list, respectively.

In fact, the functions shown in Fig. 2 will be used in our main algorithm (cf. Fig. 4). Thus, we explain the functions `merge` (lines 05–07) and e(`l`$_1$, …, `l`$_k$) (lines 08–10) a bit more in detail.

The `merge` function takes a set $\mathcal{L}$ of pairwise disjoint lists of derivations, each one in ascending order with respect to $\precsim$, and merges them into

```
   -- standard Haskell functions: list deconstructors, take operation
01 head (x:xs) = x
02 tail (x:xs) = xs
03 take n xs = []      if n == 0 or xs == []
04 take n xs = (head xs):take (n-1) (tail xs)

   -- merge operation (lists in ℒ should be disjoint)
05 merge ℒ = []      if ℒ \ {[]} = ∅
06 merge ℒ = m:merge ({tail l | l ∈ ℒ, l != [], head l == m} ∪
                      {l | l ∈ ℒ, l != [], head l != m})
07      where m = min{head l | l ∈ ℒ, l != []}

   -- top concatenation
08 e(l_1,...,l_k) = []      if l_i == [] for some i ∈ {1,...,k}
09 e(l_1,...,l_k) = e(head l_1,...,head l_k):merge {e(l^i_1,...,l^i_k) | i ∈ {1,...,k}}
                    ⎧ l_j           if j < i
10      where l^i_j = ⎨ tail l_j      if j = i
                    ⎩ [head l_j]    if j > i
```

Figure 2: Some useful functions specified in a functional programming style.

one list with the same property (as known from the merge sort algorithm).

Note that the minimum used in line 07 is based on the linear pre-order $\precsim$. For this reason, it need not be uniquely determined. However, in an implementation this function is deterministic, depending on the the data structures.

The function $e(\mathtt{l}_1, \ldots, \mathtt{l}_k)$ implements the top-concatenation with e on lists of derivations. It is defined for every $e = (v_1 \ldots v_k, \sigma, v) \in E$ and takes lists $\mathtt{l}_1, \ldots, \mathtt{l}_k$ of derivations, each in ascending order as for `merge`. The resulting list is also in ascending order.

4 Algorithm

In this section, we develop our algorithm for solving the n-best-derivations problem. We begin by motivating our general approach, which amounts to solving the 1-best-derivation problem first and then extending that solution to a solution of the n-best-derivations problem.

It can be shown that for every $m \geq n$, the set $\min_n(H_v)$ is equal to the set of all prefixes of length n of elements of $\min_m(H_v)$. According to this observation, we will develop a function `p` mapping every $v \in V$ to a (possibly infinite) list such that the prefix of length n is in $\min_n(H_v)$ for every n. Then, by virtue of lazy evaluation, a solution to the n-best-derivations problem can be obtained by evaluating the term

```
take n (p v)
```

where `take` is specified in lines 03–04 of Fig. 2. Thus, what is left to be done is to specify `p` appropriately.

4.1 A provisional specification of p

Consider the following provisional specification of `p`:

$$\mathtt{p\ v} = \mathtt{merge}\ \{e(\mathtt{p\ v}_1, \ldots, \mathtt{p\ v}_k) \mid e = (v_1 \ldots v_k, \sigma, v) \in E\} \quad (\dagger)$$

where the functions `merge` and $e(\mathtt{l}_1, \ldots, \mathtt{l}_k)$ are specified in lines 05–07 and lines 08–10 of Fig. 2, respectively. This specification models exactly the trivial equation

$$H_v = \bigcup_{e=(v_1 \ldots v_k, \sigma, v) \in E} e(H_{v_1}, \ldots, H_{v_k})$$

for every $v \in V$, where the union and the top-concatenation have been implemented for lists via the functions `merge` and $e(\mathtt{l}_1, \ldots, \mathtt{l}_k)$.

This specification is adequate if H is acyclic. For cyclic hypergraphs however, it can not even solve the 1-best-derivation problem. To illustrate this, we consider the hypergraph of Ex. 2 and calculate[6]

$$\begin{aligned}
&\texttt{take 1 (p 1)} \\
&= \texttt{(head (p 1)):take 0 (tail (p 1))} \quad (04)\\
&= \texttt{head (p 1)} \quad (03)\\
&= \texttt{head (merge } \{e_1(), e_2(), e_3(\texttt{p 1})\}\texttt{)} \quad (\dagger)\\
&= \min\{\texttt{head } e_1(), \texttt{head } e_2(), \texttt{head } e_3(\texttt{p 1})\} \quad (01, 06, 07)\\
&= \min\{\texttt{head } e_1(), \texttt{head } e_2(), e_3(\texttt{head (p 1)})\}. \quad (09)
\end{aligned}$$

Note that the infinite regress occurs because the computation of the head element `head (p 1)` depends on itself. This leads us to the idea of "pulling" this head element (which is the solution to the 1-best-derivation problem) "out" of the merge in (†). Applying this idea to our particular example, we reach the following equation for `p 1`:

$$\texttt{p 1} = e_2\texttt{: merge } \{e_1(), e_3(\texttt{p 1})\}$$

because e_2 is the best derivation in H_1. Then, in order to evaluate `merge` we have to compute

$$\begin{aligned}
&\min\{\texttt{head } e_1(), \texttt{head } e_3(\texttt{p 1})\}\\
&= \min\{e_1, e_3(\texttt{head (p 1)})\}\\
&= \min\{e_1, e_3(e_2)\}.
\end{aligned}$$

Since $h(e_1) = h(e_3(e_2)) = 4$, we can choose any of them, say e_1, and continue:

$$\begin{aligned}
&e_2\texttt{: merge } \{e_1(), e_3(\texttt{p 1})\}\\
&= e_2\texttt{: } e_1\texttt{: merge } \{\texttt{tail } e_1(), e_3(\texttt{p 1})\}\\
&= e_2\texttt{: } e_1\texttt{: } e_3(e_2)\texttt{: merge } \{\texttt{tail } e_3(\texttt{p 1})\}\\
&= \dots
\end{aligned}$$

Generalizing this example, the function p could be specified as follows:

$$\texttt{p 1 = (b 1) : merge } \{exp\} \qquad (\dagger\dagger)$$

where `b 1` evaluates the 1-best derivation in H_1 and exp "somehow" calculates the next best derivations. In the following subsection, we elaborate this approach. First, we develop an algorithm for solving the 1-best-derivation problem.

4.2 Solving the 1-best-derivation problem

Using SP and CP, it can be shown that for every $v \in V$ such that $H_v \neq \emptyset$ there is a minimal derivation in H_v which does not contain any subderivation in H_v (apart from itself). In other words, it is not necessary to consider cycles when solving the 1-best-derivation problem.

[6]Please note that $e_1()$ is an application of the function in lines 08–10 of Fig. 2 while e_1 is a derivation.

We can exploit this knowledge in a program by keeping a set U of visited nodes, taking care not to consider edges which lead us back to those nodes. Consider the following function:

$$\begin{aligned}
\texttt{b v U} = \min\{&e(\texttt{b } v_1 \texttt{ U'}, \dots, \texttt{b } v_k \texttt{ U'}) \mid\\
&e = (v_1 \dots v_k, \sigma, v) \in E,\\
&\{v_1, \dots, v_k\} \cap \texttt{U'} = \emptyset\}\\
\text{where } &\texttt{U'} = \texttt{U} \cup \{\texttt{v}\}
\end{aligned}$$

The argument U is the set of visited nodes. The term `b v` $\emptyset$ evaluates to a minimal element of H_v, or to $\min \emptyset$ if $H_v = \emptyset$. The problem of this divide-and-conquer (or top-down) approach is that managing a separate set U for every recursive call incurs a big overhead in the computation.

This overhead can be avoided by using a dynamic programming (or bottom-up) approach where each node is visited only once, and nodes are visited in the order of their respective best derivations.

To be more precise, we maintain a family $(P_v \mid v \in V)$ of already found best derivations (where $P_v \in \min_{\leq 1}(H_v)$ and initially empty) and a set C of candidate derivations, where candidates for all vertices are considered at the same time. In each iteration, a minimal candidate with respect to $\precsim$ is selected. This candidate is then declared the best derivation of its respective node.

The following lemma shows that the bottom-up approach is sound.

Lemma 3 *Let $(P_v \mid v \in V)$ be a family such that $P_v \in \min_{\leq 1}(H_v)$. We define*

$$C = \bigcup_{\substack{e=(v_1\dots v_k,\sigma,v)\in E,\\ P_v=\emptyset}} e(P_{v_1}, \dots, P_{v_k}) .$$

Then (i) for every $\xi \in \bigcup_{v \in V, P_v = \emptyset} H_v$ there is a $\xi' \in C$ such that $\xi' \preceq \xi$, and (ii) for every $v \in V$ and $\xi \in C \cap H_v$ the following implication holds: if $\xi \leq \xi'$ for every $\xi' \in C$, then $\xi \in \min_1(H_v)$.

An algorithm based on this lemma is shown in Fig. 3. Its key function `iter` uses the notion of accumulating parameters. The parameter q is a mapping corresponding to the family $(P_v \mid v \in V)$ of the lemma, i. e., `q v` $= P_v$; the parameter c is a set corresponding to C. We begin in line 01 with the function q0 mapping every vertex to the empty list. According to the lemma, the candidates then consist of the nullary edges.

As long as there are candidates left (line 04), in a recursive call of `iter` the parameter q is updated with the newly found pair $(v, [\xi])$ of vertex v and (list of) best derivation ξ (expressed by

Require Σ-hypergraph $H = (V, E)$, linear preorder $\precsim$ fulfilling SP and CP.
Ensure `b v` $\in \min_1(H_v)$ for every $v \in V$ such that if `b v == [`$e(\xi_1, \ldots, \xi_k)$`]` for some $e = (v_1 \ldots v_k, \sigma, v) \in E$, then `b` v_i `==` `[`ξ_i`]` for every $i \in \{1, \ldots, k\}$.

01 `b = iter q0` $\{(\varepsilon, \alpha, v) \in E \mid \alpha \in \Sigma^{(0)}\}$
02 `q0 v = []`
03 `iter q` $\emptyset$ `= q`
04 `iter q c = iter (q//(v,[`ξ`])) c'`
05 where
06 $\quad\xi$ `= min c` and $\xi \in H_v$
07 $\quad$`c' =` $\bigcup_{\substack{e=(v_1\ldots v_k,\sigma,v)\in E \\ \texttt{q } v \texttt{ == []}}} e(\texttt{q } v_1, \ldots, \texttt{q } v_k)$

Figure 3: Algorithm solving the 1-best-derivation problem.

`q//(v,[`ξ`]))` and the candidate set is recomputed accordingly. When the candidate set is exhausted (line 03), then `q` is returned.

Correctness and completeness of the algorithm follow from Statements (ii) and (i) of Lemma 3, respectively. Now we show termination. In every iteration a new next best derivation is determined and the candidate set is recomputed. This set only contains candidates for vertices $v \in V$ such that `q v == []`. Hence, after at most $|V|$ iterations the candidates must be depleted, and the algorithm terminates.

We note that the algorithm is very similar to that of Knuth (1977). However, in contrast to the latter, (i) it admits $H_v = \emptyset$ for some $v \in V$ and (ii) it computes some minimal derivation instead of the weight of some minimal derivation.

Runtime According to the literature, the runtime of Knuth's algorithm is in $O(|E| \cdot \log|V|)$ (Knuth, 1977). This statement relies on a number of optimizations which are beyond our scope. We just sketch two optimizations: (i) the candidate set can be implemented in a way which admits obtaining its minimum in $O(\log|C|)$, and (ii) for the computation of candidates, each edge needs to be considered only once during the whole run of the algorithm.

4.3 Solving the n-best-derivations problem

Being able to solve the 1-best-derivation problem, we can now refine our specification of `p`. The refined algorithm is given in Fig. 4; for the functions not given there, please refer to Fig. 3 (function `b`) and to Fig. 2 (functions `merge`, `tail`, and the top-concatenation). In particular, line 02 of Fig. 4 shows the general way of "pulling out" the head element as it was indicated in Section 4.1 via an example. We also remark that the definition of the top-concatenation (lines 08–09 of Fig. 2) corresponds to the way in which $\mathrm{mult}_{\preceq k}$ was sped up in Fig. 4 of (Huang and Chiang, 2005).

Theorem 4 *The algorithm in Fig. 4 is correct with respect to its require/ensure specification and it terminates for every input.*

PROOF (SKETCH). We indicate how induction on n can be used for the proof. If $n = 0$, then the statement is trivially true. Let $n > 0$. If `b v == []`, then the statement is trivially true as well. Now we consider the converse case. To this end, we use the following three auxiliary statements.

(1) `take n (merge` $\{$`l`$_1, \ldots,$`l`$_k\}$`) =` `take n (merge` $\{$`take n l`$_1, \ldots,$`take n l`$_k\}$`)`,

(2) `take n` $e($`l`$_1, \ldots,$`l`$_k)$ `=` `take n` $e($`take n l`$_1, \ldots,$`take n l`$_k)$,

(3) `take n (tail l) = tail (take (n+1) l)`.

Using these statements, line 04 of Fig. 2, and line 02 of Fig. 4, we are able to "pull" the `take` of `take n (p v)` "into" the right-hand side of `p v`, ultimately yielding terms of the form `take n (p v`$_j$`)` in the first line of the `merge` application and `take (n-1) (p v`$'_j$`)` in the second one.

Then we can show the following statement by induction on m (note that the n is still fixed from the outer induction): for every $m \in \mathbb{N}$ we have that if the tree in `b v` has at most height m, then `take n (p v)` $\in \min_n(H_v)$. To this end, we use the following two auxiliary statements.

(4) For every sequence of pairwise disjoint subsets $P_1, \ldots, P_k \subseteq \bigcup_{v \in V} H_v$, sequence of natural numbers $n_1, \ldots, n_k \in \mathbb{N}$, and lists $l_1 \in \min_{n_1}(P_1)$, $\ldots$, $l_k \in \min_{n_k}(P_k)$ such that $n_j \geq n$ for every $j \in \{1, \ldots, k\}$ we have that `take n (merge` $\{l_1, \ldots, l_k\}$`)` $\in \min_n(P_1 \cup \ldots \cup P_k)$.

(5) For every edge $e = (v_1 \ldots v_k, \sigma, v) \in E$, subsets $P_1, \ldots, P_k \subseteq \bigcup_{v \in V} H_v$, and lists $l_1 \in \min_n(P_1), \ldots, l_k \in \min_n(P_k)$ we have that `take n` $e(l_1, \ldots, l_k) \in \min_n(e(P_1, \ldots, P_k))$.

Using these statements, it remains to show that $\{e(\xi_1, \ldots, \xi_k)\} \circ \min_{n-1}\big((e(H_{v_1}, \ldots, H_{v_k}) \setminus \{e(\xi_1, \ldots, \xi_k)\}) \cup \bigcup_{e' \neq e} e'(H_{v'_1}, \ldots, H_{v'_k})\big) \subseteq \min_n(H_v)$ where `b v =` `[`$e(\xi_1, \ldots, \xi_k)$`]` and $\circ$ denotes language concatenation. This can be shown by using the definition of $\min_n$.

Termination of the algorithm now follows from the fact that every finite prefix of `p v` is well defined. ■

Require Σ-hypergraph $H = (V, E)$, linear pre-order $\precsim$ fulfilling SP and CP.
Ensure $\big(\texttt{take n (p v)}\big) \in \min_n(H_v)$ for every $v \in V$ and $n \in \mathbb{N}$.

01 $\texttt{p v = []} \quad$ if $\texttt{b v == []}$

02 $\texttt{p v =} \ e(\xi_1, \dots, \xi_k)\texttt{:merge (\{tail } e(\texttt{p v}_1, \dots, \texttt{p v}_k) \mid e = (v_1 \dots v_k, \sigma, v) \in E\} \cup$
$\{e'(\texttt{p v}'_1, \dots, \texttt{p v}'_k) \mid e' = (v'_1 \dots v'_k, \sigma', v) \in E,\ e' \neq e\})$
if $\texttt{b v == [}e(\xi_1, \dots, \xi_k)\texttt{]}$

Figure 4: Algorithm solving the n-best-derivations problem.

4.4 Implementation, Complexity, and Experiments

We have implemented the algorithm (consisting of Figs. 3 and 4 and the auxiliary functions of Fig. 2) in HASKELL. The implementation is rather straightforward except for the following three points.

(1) Weights: we assume that $\precsim$ is defined by means of weights (cf. Ex. 2), and that comparing these weights is in $O(1)$ (which often holds because of limited precision). Hence, we store with each derivation its weight so that comparison according to $\precsim$ is in $O(1)$ as well.

(2) Memoization: we use a memoization technique to ensure that no derivation occurring in `p v` is computed twice.

(3) Merge: the `merge` operation deserves some consideration because it is used in a nested fashion, yielding trees of `merge` applications. This leads to an undesirable runtime complexity because these trees need not be balanced. Thus, instead of actually computing the `merge` in `p` and in the top-concatenation, we just return a data structure describing what should be merged. That data structure consists of a best element and a list of lists of derivations to be merged (cf. lines 06 and 09 in Fig. 2). We use a higher-order function to manage these data structures on a heap, performing the merge in a nonnested way.

Runtime Here we consider the n-best part of the algorithm, i. e. we assume the computation of the mapping `b` to take constant time. Note however that due to memoization, `b` is only computed once. Then the runtime complexity of our implementation is in $O\big(|E| + |V| \cdot n \cdot \log(|E| + n)\big)$. This can be seen as follows.

By line 02 in Fig. 4, the initial heaps in the higher-order merge described under (3) have a total of $|E|$ elements. Building these heaps is thus in $O(|E|)$. By line 09 in Fig. 2, each newly found derivation spawns at most as many new candidates

n	total time [s]	time for n-best part [s]
1	8.713	—
25 000	10.832	2.119
50 000	12.815	4.102
100 000	16.542	7.739
200 000	24.216	15.503

Table 1: Experimental results

on the heap as the maximum rank in Σ. We assume this to be constant. Moreover, at most n derivations are computed for each node, that is, at most $|V| \cdot n$ in total. Hence, the size of the heap of a node is in $O(|E| + n)$. For each derivation we compute, we have to pop the minimal element off the heap (cf. line 07 in Fig. 2), which is in $O\big(\log(|E| + n)\big)$, and we have to compute the union of the remaining heap with the newly spawned candidates, which has the same complexity.

We give another estimate for the total number of derivations computed by the algorithm, which is based on the following observation. When popping a new derivation ξ off the heap, new next best candidates are computed. This involves computing at most as many new derivations as the number of nodes of ξ, because for each hyperedge occurring in ξ we have to consider the next best alternative. Since we pop off at most n elements from the heap belonging to the target node, we arrive at the estimate $d \cdot n$, where d is the size of the biggest derivation of said node.

A slight improvement of the runtime complexity can be obtained by restricting the heap size to n best elements, as argued by Huang and Chiang (2005). This way, they are able to obtain the complexity $O(|E| + d \cdot n \cdot \log n)$.

We have conducted experiments on an Intel Core Duo 1200 MHz with 2 GB of RAM using a cyclic hypergraph containing 671 vertices and 12136 edges. The results are shown in Table 1. This table indicates that the runtime of the n-best part is roughly linear in n.

References

Athanasios Alexandrakis and Symeon Bozapalidis. 1987. Weighted grammars and Kleene's theorem. *Inform. Process. Lett.*, 24(1):1–4.

Jean Berstel and Christophe Reutenauer. 1982. Recognizable formal power series on trees. *Theoret. Comput. Sci.*, 18(2):115–148.

Matthias Büchse, Jonathan May, and Heiko Vogler. 2009. Determinization of weighted tree automata using factorizations. Talk presented at FSMNLP 09 in Pretoria, South Africa.

Zoltán Ésik and Werner Kuich. 2003. Formal tree series. *J. Autom. Lang. Comb.*, 8(2):219–285.

Zoltán Fülöp and Heiko Vogler. 2009. Weighted tree automata and tree transducers. In Manfred Droste, Werner Kuich, and Heiko Vogler, editors, *Handbook of Weighted Automata*, chapter 9. Springer.

Joshua Goodman. 1999. Semiring parsing. *Comp. Ling.*, 25(4):573–605.

Liang Huang and David Chiang. 2005. Better k-best parsing. In *Parsing '05: Proceedings of the Ninth International Workshop on Parsing Technology*, pages 53–64. ACL.

Dan Klein and Christopher D. Manning. 2001. Parsing and hypergraphs. In *Proceedings of IWPT*, pages 123–134.

Donald E. Knuth. 1977. A Generalization of Dijkstra's Algorithm. *Inform. Process. Lett.*, 6(1):1–5, February.

Zhifei Li, Jason Eisner, and Sanjeev Khudanpur. 2009. Variational decoding for statistical machine translation. In *Proc. ACL-IJCNLP '09*, pages 593–601. ACL.

Andreas Maletti and Giorgio Satta. 2009. Parsing algorithms based on tree automata. In *Proc. 11th Int. Conf. Parsing Technologies*, pages 1–12. ACL.

Jonathan May and Kevin Knight. 2006. A better n-best list: practical determinization of weighted finite tree automata. In *Proc. HLT*, pages 351–358. ACL.

Mark-Jan Nederhof. 2003. Weighted deductive parsing and Knuth's algorithm. *Comp. Ling.*, 29(1):135–143.

Lars Relund Nielsen, Kim Allan Andersen, and Daniele Pretolani. 2005. Finding the k shortest hyperpaths. *Comput. Oper. Res.*, 32(6):1477–1497.

Franz Josef Och and Hermann Ney. 2002. Discriminative training and maximum entropy models for statistical machine translation. In *ACL*, pages 295–302.

Adam Pauls and Dan Klein. 2009. k-best a* parsing. In *Proc. ACL-IJCNLP '09*, pages 958–966, Morristown, NJ, USA. ACL.

J. W. Thatcher. 1967. Characterizing derivation trees of context-free grammars through a generalization of finite automata theory. *J. Comput. Syst. Sci.*, 1(4):317–322.

Author Index

Association for Computational Linguistics
209 N. Eighth Street
Stroudsburg, Pennsylvania 18360

CURRAN ASSOCIATES INC
proceedings.com

Knowledge and Reasoning for Language Processing 2006

(KRAQ 06)

Held at EACL 2006

Trento, Italy
3 April 2006

ISBN: 978-1-61738-486-8